COVID 19

COVID 19
CONTAGION, CONTENTION, RECUPERATION

Gerald L. Hutson

XULON PRESS

Xulon Press
2301 Lucien Way #415
Maitland, FL 32751
407.339.4217
www.xulonpress.com

Printed in the United States of America.

Paperback ISBN-13: 978-1-6322-1766-0
eBook ISBN-13: 978-1-6322-1767-7

As an American with a loving wife and family, I say with a heavy heart, how sorry I feel for those who have suffered deaths or have been through the long task of surviving the COVID-19 virus. There is no words or long speech that can be given to those who have felt this pain. My heart every day feels hurt when I see the suffering of patients in hospitals and those on ventilators with the hope of survival. To all the parents, grandparents, children, grandchildren, aunts, uncles, cousins, and many more friends who have lost their loved ones to this virus, there is no replacement for a lost loved one. I only wish there was a way to compensate for everyone's suffering.

Love and Kindness-Gerald L. Hutson

Author's Introduction

Today is Monday, August 17th, 2020, a beautiful blue-sky morning, temperature 81 degrees, much cooler than previous days. I am going through my usual morning routine of feeding the dog and cat and turning on the TV to see what the latest news is reporting about the COVID-19 Coronavirus pandemic that is expanding rapidly in the United States.

COVID-19 has been a concern of mine since I first heard about the virus spreading and killing thousands in China and around the world. The United States became part of this spread when I began following and documenting the impact of this virus. COVID-19 is serious and is growing throughout the world, including the United States. When COVID-19 was growing and killing thousands, the news of the virus spread rapidly through the media and worldwide, which included the New York Times, Wall Street Journal, and other media sources that reported the spread of the pandemic virus to the American people.

In this book, I will discuss the Chinese government and how they struggled in late January to cope with a worsening coronavirus epidemic as its official numbers of infections soared 50% in one day, and additional cases appeared in the United States. The government of Beijing broadened an extraordinary quarantine to 50 million people, roughly equal to the population of Spain. It enforced a travel ban on 16 cities in Central Hubei Province, where the lethal virus first appeared.

The U.S. Health officials confirmed three new cases in late January 2020, one in Arizona and two in California, bringing the total to five in the United States. According to the Centers for Disease Control and Prevention, the patients in Chicago and Washington state traveled to Wuhan, China, and all were hospitalized.

The U.S. Health officials expected more American cases as of late January 2020. Nancy Messonnier, director of CDC's National Center for Immunization and Respiratory Diseases, said, "The threat is serious, and public health response is aggressive with the aim of helping to protect Americans."

Throughout this book, you can read and envision the progress of the virus, which started in China and spread rapidly to other countries, including the United States. China was faced with a pandemic that was killing thousands quickly and had to respond. Still, like the United States, at the beginning of COVID-19, they were unprepared to confront the virus, facing the need for personal protective equipment and hospital space to handle the virus.

While suffering was continuing worldwide, the president of the United States had appeared to have other interests that were of more concern than the surging COVID-19 virus reaching the United States. America was not ready, and President Donald Trump and his administration were not prepared, which would eventually take thousands of Americans' lives.

With the COVID-19 virus threatening the world and beginning to filter into the United States, and killing hundreds in China, there was no word mentioned by Trump about the pandemic that was spreading in low numbers to other countries. President Donald Trump was delighting in his impeachment acquittal on February 6th, unleashing his fury against those who tried to remove him. The first alarm sounded in early January 2020, with an outbreak of a novel coronavirus in China that would ignite a global pandemic. The Trump administration squandered for nearly two months, which could have been used to bolster the federal stockpile of critically needed medical supplies and equipment. Federal purchasing contractors waited until mid-March 2020 to begin placing orders of N95 respiratory masks, mechanical ventilators, and other equipment required by front line healthcare workers.

As of June 30, 2020, COVID-19 Coronavirus cases have reached over 2 million, with over 125 thousand American deaths. COVID-19 Coronavirus in the world, including the United States, reached over 10 million cases with over 500 thousand deaths. The COVID-19 virus is with us and will continue to spread unless the leaders of our country accept that this virus is real and the preparedness of the American people follow the directions laid down by the Trump administration and Vice President Pence and his Coronavirus team. The President of the United States, Donald Trump, has been pushing the states to open, by passing the Three-Phase Plan. Trump's main concern was on the economy, jobs, and bringing the states back to full recovery. He was not as concerned with implementing strategies outlined by his Coronavirus team and advice from Dr. Fauci, which forecasted that if we don't follow the plan of wearing masks, social distancing, and staying home, the virus will spread, and thousands of lives will be lost.

Table of Contents

Timeline of Coronavirus COVID-19

December 2019-August 2020

31 Dec. 2019
- China alerts the World Health Organization (W.H.O.) about a sudden outpouring of pneumonia-like cases in Wuhan.

1 Jan. 2020
- The seafood market (Hunan Seafood Wholesale Market) was identified as a suspected center of the outbreak closed.

3 Jan. 2020
- China officially notifies the W.H.O. of an outbreak.

6-8 Jan. 2020
- CDC issues a series of warnings and alerts for Americans on travel.

9 Jan. 2020
- The W.H.O. says a new type of coronavirus causes the infection.

10 Jan. 2020
- China shares the genetic code of the new virus.

11 Jan. 2020
- Scientists start working on a vaccine, and the first death is confirmed.

13 Jan. 2020
- The virus spreads abroad for the first time, with a case in Thailand.

14 Jan. 2020
- Wuhan, China, implements screening methods for passenger terminals.

16 Jan. 2020	• Japan reports its first case, a man in his mid-30's who did not visit the seafood market.
17 Jan. 2020	• A second man dies at age 69 in Wuhan.
18 Jan. 2020	• A third person dies from coronavirus in Wuhan.
18 Jan. 2020	• Secretary of Health and Human Services Alex Azar first briefed Trump about the virus via phone.
20 Jan. 2020	• China confirms fourth death, an 89-year-old man. Chinese state TV confirms the human-to-human transmission of the disease.
21 Jan. 2020	• The United States confirms the first case in Washington state, a man who traveled to the Wuhan area.
	• Trump: "Totally under control, it's one person coming in from China, and we have it under control. It's going to be just fine."
22 Jan. 2020	• Speaking to CNBC in Davos, Switzerland, Trump dismissed the virus. "We have it totally under control."
22 Jan. 2020	• Chinese officials confirm the virus may mutate
	• Chinese CDC confirms a total of 440 cases in mainland China and nine deaths.
	• W.H.O. meets to discuss whether to declare an international health emergency.

23 Jan. 2020	• China CDC confirms 571 cases in mainland China and 17 deaths.
	• China extends travel restrictions or quarantines to five cities.
	• Singapore confirms its first case.
24 Jan. 2020	• The United States confirms its second case, a woman in her sixties in Chicago.
	• Chinese CDC confirms 830 cases and 25 deaths.
	• China extends travel restrictions to 12 cities.
	• Wuhan construction crews building two hospitals to treat patients of the outbreak.
25 Jan. 2020	• The United States confirms its third case, a man in his fifties in California.
26 Jan. 2020	• The United States confirms its fourth and fifth cases in Los Angeles and Arizona.
27 Jan. 2020	• The United States extends screening to twenty airports.
27 Jan. 2020	• Top White House aides met about the virus with one warning that an outbreak could cost Trump his re-election.
28 Jan. 2020	• Trade advisor Peter Navarro wrote in a memo that the virus could cause mass loss of life and economic destruction.
	• The U.S. coronavirus task force was created.

30 Jan. 2020	• The United States issues a Level 4 travel advisory for all China.
	• The W.H.O. declares the coronavirus outbreak as a Public Health Emergency of International Concern (PHEIC)
	• Germany finds evidence of asymptomatic transmission of the coronavirus.
	• The United States confirms its sixth case, the first person-to-person transmission of the virus in the country.
31 Jan. 2020	• Trump banned entry into the U.S. for most foreigners who had been in China, though by then, there were already cases in the United States, and the ban exempted Americans who had been in China.
1 Feb. 2020	• The United States confirms its eighth case.
2 Feb. 2020	• The United States confirms its ninth, tenth, and eleventh case.
	• The United States completed a second round of evacuations from Wuhan.
	• CDC announces several planes carrying passengers from Wuhan, China, will arrive in California, Texas, and Nebraska.
	• CDC begins shipping diagnostic test kits to more than a hundred labs in the United States.
	• U.S. Peace Corps evacuates all volunteers out of China.

6 Feb. 2020
- An American citizen with the coronavirus dies in Wuhan, becoming the first known American death from the outbreak.
- W.H.O. convenes a global research end innovation forum to accelerate research and action on the coronavirus.

7 Feb. 2020
- Donald Trump and China's Xi Jinping speak about the coronavirus, with Trump praising China's efforts and pledging support.
- The United States pledges $100 million to assist China and other countries to fight coronavirus.

10 Feb. 2020
- The United States confirms its thirteenth case.
- The Trump administration budget proposal for FY21 would sharply cut funding for W.H.O. and global health funding.

12 Feb. 2020
- The United States confirms its fourteenth case.
- Some U.S. states find testing kits distributed by CDC deliver "inconclusive results."

13 Feb. 2020
- The United States confirms the fifteenth case of coronavirus.

21 Feb. 2020
- The United States confirms a total of thirty-four coronavirus cases, including passengers evacuated from the Diamond Princess Cruise Ship.

25 Feb. 2020
- Nancy Messonnier of the National Center for Immunization and Respiratory Diseases warned that "disruption to everyday life may be severe" due to the virus. Trump was reportedly furious that Messonnier had needlessly scared the public. He did not recommend social distancing until March 16th. In addition, it was reported that American officials embedded at the W.H.O., which Trump has since blamed for covering up the outbreak, were feeding information about the coronavirus to Washington starting late 2019.

26 Feb. 2020
- President Trump names Vice President Mike Pence to lead the U.S. coronavirus response team.
- W.H.O. announces that February 25th was the first day there were more new cases outside of China than from China itself.

27 Feb. 2020

- U.S. CDC widens its testing guidelines.
- The W.H.O. Director-General discussed preparedness for COVID-19 and listed questions every health minister worldwide should be able to answer, including the United States.
- Are we ready for the first case?
- Do we have enough medical oxygen ventilators and other vital equipment?
- How will we know if there are cases in other areas of the country?
- Do our health workers have the training and equipment they need to be safe?
- Do we have the right measures at airports and border crossings to test people who are sick?
- Do our labs have the right chemicals that allow them to test samples?
- Are we ready to treat patients with severe or critical disease?
- Do our hospitals and clinics have the right procedures to prevent and control infections?
- Do our people have the right information?
- Do they know what the disease looks like?

28 Feb. 2020	• The W.H.O. Director-General said we don't need to wait for vaccines and therapeutics. There are things every individual can do to protect themselves and others Immediately (Today).
	• Clean your hands regularly with an alcohol-based hand rub or wash them with soap and water.
	• Touching your face after touching contaminated surfaces or sick people is one way the coronavirus can be transmitted.
29 Feb. 2020	• The United States reports its first death, a man in his fifties with an underlying health condition.
	• The stock market tumbles.
1 March 2020	• The United States reports its second death, a man in his seventies with underlying health conditions.
	• Florida declares a state of emergency.
	• The global death toll surpasses 3,000.
2 March 2020	• The United States reports four more deaths, all in Washington state.
4 March 2020	• California declares a state of emergency over coronavirus.
5 March 2020	• New Jersey reports its first case.
	• Maryland declares a state of emergency.

6 March 2020	• The number of coronavirus cases hit 100,000 globally.
	• Kentucky confirms first case.
	• Oklahoma announces first case.
	• CDC urges those over 60 to stay indoors.
7 March 2020	• New York declares a state of emergency.
	• DC reports first positive coronavirus case.
	• Kansas reports first positive coronavirus case.
8 March 2020	• The first three positive coronavirus cases reported in Iowa.
	• Connecticut confirms first case of coronavirus.
	• The number of cases in the U.S. passes 500.
	• Eight U.S. states declare a state of emergency.
9 March 2020	• W.H.O. reports that more than 70% of coronavirus cases in China have recovered.
	• Rhode Island declares a state of emergency.
	• Louisiana reports first positive coronavirus case.
	• New York announces it will be making its own hand sanitizer using prison labor.

10 March 2020
- New Jersey reports the first coronavirus death.
- Pence announces no copays on coronavirus treatment.
- South Dakota reports the first coronavirus death.
- Twenty-three total states all declare a state of emergency.

11 March 2020
- W.H.O. declares the coronavirus outbreak a pandemic.
- Arizona and Washington DC declared a state of emergency.
- United States announces level 3 travel advisory and suspended entry to all foreign nationals traveling from China, Iran, and certain European countries at any point during the 14 days before their scheduled travel to the U.S.
- North Dakota records its first positive case of coronavirus.
- Delaware records its first positive case of coronavirus.

12 March 2020
- Kansas reports first coronavirus death.
- Montana declares a state of emergency.
- Virginia declares a state of emergency.
- New York City declares a state of emergency.

13 March 2020	• Donald Trump declares a State of National Emergency under the Stafford Act.
	• Sixteen states announce school closures.
	• W.H.O. declares Europe the new epi-center of the coronavirus outbreak.
14 March 2020	• The United States reaches 2,750 coronavirus cases; all states have reported cases except West Virginia.
	• Georgia declares a state of emergency.
	• Virginia reports first coronavirus death.
	• New York records its first coronavirus related death.
15 March 2020	• Oklahoma declares a state of emergency.
	• Maine declares a state of emergency.
16 March 2020	• CDC reports over 4,000 coronavirus cases in the U.S.
	• South Carolina reports first coronavirus death.
17 March 2020	• West Virginia confirms its first coronavirus case, making the virus present in all 50 states.
18 March 2020	• Trump signs the Families Coronavirus Response Act into law.
	• Maryland reports first coronavirus death.

19 March 2020	• China reports zero new local coronavirus infections.
	• Vermont reports first coronavirus related death.
	• The U.S. CDC reports more than 13,000 coronavirus cases.
20 March 2020	• The United States CDC reports more than 18,000 coronavirus cases.
	• Ohio reports first coronavirus death.
	• Washington, DC, reports first coronavirus death.
	• Trump invokes Defense Production Act to disperse medical supplies to hospitals.
21 March 2020	• China reports no new local coronavirus cases for the third consecutive day.
	• Arizona records first coronavirus death.
22 March 2020	• Global coronavirus cases double from last week, reaching almost 330,000 cases.
23 March 2020	• New Hampshire reports first coronavirus death.
	W.H.O. announces the "pandemic is • accelerating."
24 March 2020	• The United States reaches 50,000 coronavirus cases.
25 March 2020	• North Carolina reports first coronavirus death
	• W.H.O. warns that there is a "significant shortage" of medical supplies.

26 March 2020	• United States' death toll reaches one thousand.
	• New York City becomes the epicenter of the U.S. coronavirus outbreak; cases are doubling every three days.
27 March 2020	• Montana reports first coronavirus death.
28 March 2020	• Global deaths surpass 30,000.
29 March 2020	• The United States passes 140,000 coronavirus cases, more than any other country in the world.
	• President Trump extends social distancing guidelines until April 30th.
30 March 2020	• President Trump announces more than 1 million Americans have been tested for coronavirus.
31 March 2020	• The United States unveils a model that projects that 100,000 Americans could die from the coronavirus.
2 April 2020	• Global coronavirus cases pass the one million mark; deaths exceed 50,000.
	• The White House encourages all Americans to wear masks in public.
3 April 2020	• U.S. President Donald Trump invokes the Defense Production Act to halt the export of masks and other personal protection equipment.
	• The United States confirms 32,000 new cases in one day, setting a record for the most massive jump in daily cases.

4 April 2020	• Without scientific evidence, President Donald Trump endorses the Malaria drug, hydroxychloroquine, as an effective coronavirus treatment.
5 April 2020	• The United States reports 1,300 coronavirus deaths in one day, its highest spike.
6 April 2020	• United States death toll passes 10,000. • China reports no new coronavirus deaths for the first time since January.
10 April 2020	• New York City reports more coronavirus cases than any country. • World coronavirus deaths surpass 100,000.
14 April 2020	• President Donald Trump delays thousands of stimulus checks in an unprecedented move to mandate that his name appears on the check.
15 April 2020	• President Trump delays funding to the W.H.O.
16 April 2020	• President Donald Trump unveils a set of guidelines for opening up America, giving liberty to state governors to choose whether they want to lift restrictions statewide or on a county by county basis.
17 April 2020	• U.S. Vice President Mike Pence declares that the country has enough tests for a phase one opening.
22 April 2020	• Hydroxychloroquine is deemed ineffective as a treatment against the coronavirus.

23 April 2020	• President Donald Trump erroneously recommends ingesting disinfectants to fight coronavirus. Lysol and other companies warn against this practice.
24 April 2020	• The United States coronavirus death toll passes 50,000.
	• The Federal Drug Administration warns against the use of hydroxychloroquine, an anti-malarial drug touted by President Donald Trump as a coronavirus treatment.
28 April 2020	• The United States records over one million coronavirus cases.
5 May 2020	• Trump administration considers phasing out the coronavirus task force.
	• The number of coronavirus cases globally surpasses 3.5 million.
10 May 2020	• The global total of cases reaches 4 million.
11 May 2020	• Hydroxychloroquine is proven ineffective as a treatment agent for coronavirus.
	• Two White House staff members test positive for the virus.
18 May 2020	• President Donald Trump announces he is taking hydroxychloroquine.
27 May 2020	• Coronavirus deaths in the United States pass 100,000.
	• France revokes approval of hydroxychloroquine as a potential treatment for the virus.

28 May 2020	• W.H.O. Director announces the COVID-19 pandemic is responsible for 159,000 excess deaths in 24 European countries since early March 2020.
29 May 2020	• Thirty countries and multiple international partners and institutions launched the COVID-19 (C-TAP), an initiative to make vaccines, tests, treatments, and other health technologies to fight COVID-19 accessible to all.
2 June 2020	• The Executive Director of W.H.O. Health emergencies Program addressed a High-Level Pledging Conference, organized to support the humanitarian response and alleviate suffering in the country.
5 June 2020	• W.H.O. published updated guidance on the use of masks for control of COVID-19.
13 June 2020	• W.H.O. reported that Chinese authorities had provided information on a cluster of COVID-19 cases.
16 June 2020	• The W.H.O. welcomed initial clinical trial results from the U.K., which showed dexamethasone, a corticosteroid, as a lifesaving drug for COVID-19 patients.

17 June 2020	• W.H.O. announced the hydroxychloroquine arm of solidarity trail to find an effective COVID-19 treatment. It showed that hydroxychloroquine did not reduce mortality for hospitalized COVID-19 patients.
20 June 2020	• Florida and South Carolina report sharp spikes in new cases, breaking single-day records for the third day in a row.
22 June 2020	• Citing pandemic concerns, President Trump issues restrictions on immigration to the United States, suspending most H1B, H2B, and H4 Visas.
	• More than 20 public health officials in the United States have resigned or left their posts in recent weeks.
23 June 2020	• FDA warns against the use of hand sanitizers containing methanol, a toxic substance.
24 June 2020	• Twenty-six U.S. states see a rise in coronavirus cases since easing up on lockdown restrictions.
	• The United States reports its highest daily total of new coronavirus cases.
	• New York, New Jersey, and Connecticut require visitors from "hotspot" states to self-quarantine for fourteen days.

26 June 2020
- The United States sees its highest daily increase in confirmed coronavirus cases.
- Over half of U.S. states report record numbers of new daily cases.

27 June 2020
- Twelve U.S. states slow reopening measures as new cases increase across the country.

30 June 2020
- The United States acquires over 500,000 doses of Remdesivir from Gilead.

1 July 2020
- Texas Governor Greg Abbott mandates face masks in public.

2 July 2020
- Florida reports over 10,000 new coronavirus cases, marking a new single-day record for the state.

3 July 2020
- The United States reports over 55,000 new coronavirus cases, marking a new daily record.

5 July 2020
- Florida and Texas report new single-day records for coronavirus cases.
- Scientists from over thirty countries call on W.H.O. to direct attention to evidence suggesting the airborne spread of coronavirus.

6 July 2020
- California orders six additional counties to close indoor operations for restaurants, bars, and other businesses as coronavirus cases increase in the state.

7 July 2020
- President Donald Trump formally notifies Congress and the United Nations of U.S. withdrawal from W.H.O.
- W.H.O. acknowledges evidence suggesting airborne coronavirus transmission and cautions need for further assessment.

9 July 2020
- Single-day records are reported across four states in the United States.
- W.H.O. announces an Independent Panel for Pandemic Preparedness and Response (IPPR) to evaluate the world's response to the COVID-19 pandemic.
- Louisiana mandates masks statewide amid rising cases and hospitalizations.

10 July 2020
- The United States reports 63,247 new coronavirus cases, its highest single-day increase to date.
- President Donald Trump makes his first public appearance wearing a face mask.

13 July 2020
- New York City reports no new coronavirus deaths in 24 hours.
- California's two largest public-school districts Los Angeles and San Diego announced they would be online-only for the fall semester.

14 July 2020
- The White House orders hospitals to bypass the CDC and send COVID-19 case data directly to Washington.

15 July 2020	• Single-day tallies for cases, hospitalizations, and deaths reach highs across several states, including Florida, Oklahoma, and Mississippi. • Walmart, the world's largest retailer, requires all shoppers to wear face masks in all 5,000 stores.
16 July 2020	• Georgia's governor issues an executive order rescinding mask mandates made by local governments across the state. • The FDA issues its first use authorization for COVID-19 pool testing.
21 July 2020	• The United States accuses China of hacking COVID-19 vaccine research trials.
22 July 2020	• Global coronavirus cases surpass 15 million. The United States remains the nation with the highest number of cases worldwide. • Washington, D.C. issues a new mask mandate as cases arise.
25 July 2020	• COVID-19 hospitalizations in Florida are up 79% in three weeks.
27 July 2020	• A domestic cat becomes the first animal in the United Kingdom to test positive for the virus. • Mississippi has the highest COVID-19 positivity rate in the United States.
29 July 2020	• Russia reports its on-track to approve the first COVID-19 vaccine in mid-August.

1 August 2020	• Mexico's COVID-19 death toll becomes the third highest in the world.
7 August 2020	• New York Governor Andrew Cuomo announces New York City schools can reopen in the fall if COVID-19 cases remain low.
10 August 2020	• Moderna and the Trump administration negotiate a deal to supply the United States with 100 million doses of its experimental COVID-19 vaccine.
11 August 2020	• Russia becomes the first country to approve a COVID-19 vaccine, called 'Sputnik V.' Scientists worldwide condemn the vaccine for safety reasons.
12 August 2020	• New Jersey announces schools can reopen in the fall.
13 August 2020	• The World Health Organization reports that the COVID-19 pandemic is costing the global economy $375 billion per month, citing International Monetary Fund research.
	• U.S. presidential candidate Joe Biden calls for a three-month national masks mandate.
15 August 2020	• The World Health Organization reports 294,237 new COVID-19 cases, a record number reported within 24 hours.
	• Russia begins the production of the Sputnik V COVID-19 vaccine.

17 August 2020   •   New York Governor Andrew Cuomo announces the COVID-19 infection rate below 1% for the tenth consecutive day.

Chapter 1

President Donald Trump's Response to the American People.

President Trump made his first public comments about the coronavirus on January 22nd, in a CNBC television interview. The first American case was announced the day before the interview. Trump was asked, "Are there worries about a pandemic at this point?" Trump responded by saying, "No, not at all, it's one person coming in from China, and we have it under control, it's going to be just fine." At this point, the seriousness of the virus was becoming more transparent, and Trump faced a series of choices in the weeks to follow. He could have taken aggressive measures to slow the spread of the virus and insisted on ramping up efforts to produce test kits. Trump could have urged Americans, especially older Americans, to take precautions. He could have used his power as president to reduce the number of people who would ultimately get sick.

In late January, experts were warning that the virus was spreading and that the United States needed to expand its capacity of testing to protect the American people. Newspapers wrote about the need to act now to prevent an American epidemic. President Donald Trump, with all the media covering the epidemic and possibly spreading in the United States, repeatedly told Americans that there was no reason to worry. On January 24th, he tweeted, "It will all work out well." On January 28th, he retweeted a headline from One America News, an outlet with a history of spreading false conspiracy theories: "Johnson & Johnson to create coronavirus vaccine."

Trump did take one piece of aggressive action during this time, by barring most foreigners who had recently visited China from entering the United States. Even with this done, Trump overstated the policy impact, saying he had "pretty much shut it down coming in from China." The CDC began shipping coronavirus test kits to laboratories on February 5th, as they needed to control the outbreak. But the tests did not produce reliable results, labs discovered. What is less understandable, experts say, is why the Trump administration officials were so lax about finding a reliable testing process, even as other countries were creating reliable tests.

Trump spent the first few weeks of February saying that the problem was going away. "Looks like by April, you know, in theory, when it gets warmer, it miraculously goes away," he said. In late February, Trump seemed uninterested in the virus and its impact on the American people. Trump's interest turned to other significant happenings, other than the virus; the statistics he was more interested in were the stock market indexes, which mattered significantly to him. With the market indexes falling and reaching low levels, Trump began blaming others, including CNN and MSNBC, for "panicking markets" and Democrats for their "open borders" policy. Trump continued to claim the situation was improving. "It's going to disappear," he said, "One day it's like a miracle, it will disappear."

Almost twenty years ago, during George W. Bush's presidency, the federal government developed guidelines for communicating during a public health crisis. The Trump administration is not following what previous presidents enacted. Trump, instead, suggested on many occasions that the virus was less severe than the flu. Administration officials made many false statements about the availability of tests. "Anybody that wants a test can get a test," Trump said while visiting the CDC. On March 11, Trump gave an Oval Office address meant to convey seriousness. It included some valuable advice, like the importance of handwashing. But he continued his old patterns of self-congratulation, blame-shifting, and misinformation. Trump in mid-March seemed to understand that the coronavirus is not going away anytime soon, in which he views it as a public health emergency for the country. Trump continued to brag about the relatively low number of diagnosed cases of the virus and deaths from it in America. Trump has always been obsessed with dodging blame and claiming glory that he has consistently attempted to bend the truth to his better. But this did change the impact of the virus on the American people and the world.

Seeking to reassure the American public, President Donald Trump, on February 29, 2020, said there is "no reason to panic" as the new coronavirus claimed its first victim inside the United States. Trump spoke moments after the death in Washington state was announced, taking a more measured approach a day after he complained that the virus threat was being overblown and that his political enemies were perpetrating a "hoax." "This is very serious stuff," he said. However, he still insisted on the criticism of his administration's handling of the virus outbreak was a "hoax." Trump noted that healthy Americans should recover if they contact the new virus, as he tried to reassure Americans and global markets spooked by the virus threat.

Trump spoke a day after he had denounced criticism of his response to the threat as a "hoax" cooked up by his political enemies. Speaking at a rally in South Carolina, he accused Democrats of "politicizing" the coronavirus threat and boasted about preventative steps he has ordered in an attempt to keep the virus from spreading across the United States. Those steps include barring entry by most foreign nationals who had recently visited China.

"They tried the impeachment hoax. This is their new hoax," Trump said of Democratic denunciations of his administrations' coronavirus response. Some Democrats have said Trump should have acted sooner to bolster the U.S. response to the virus.

China, on January 28, 2020, reported more than 2,700 infections and 82 deaths from the coronavirus, and some experts say there could be hundreds of thousands of cases not yet confirmed. The outbreak exposes the vulnerabilities of China's top-down government, and the damage is spreading far beyond the mainland. Scientists suspect the virus originated in November or December at Wuhan's Hunan Seafood Wholesale Market. The National Health Commission confirmed only last week that the virus could be transmitted between humans. The delay allowed the disease to spread rapidly as the medical staff took fewer precautions. One patient with coronavirus reportedly infected 14 hospital staff members in Wuhan. Epidemiologists estimate that each infected individual will transmit the illness to two or three others. "Super-Spreaders," such as doctors, can pass the bug to more than a dozen.

On January 29, 2020, countries began evacuating their citizens from the Chinese city hardest hit by the outbreak of a new virus that has killed 132 people and infected more than 6,000 on the mainland and abroad. China's latest figures cover the previous 24 hours and add 26 to the number of deaths, 25 of which were in the central province of Hubei and its capital, Wuhan, the epicenter of the outbreak. The 5,974 cases on the mainland marked a rise of 1,459 from the previous day. Dozens of infections of the new type of coronavirus have been confirmed outside mainland China as well.

China cut off access to Wuhan and 16 other cities in Hubei province to prevent people from leaving and spreading the virus further. The lockdown trapped more than 50 million people in the most far-reaching disease control measures ever imposed. On January 28, 2020, Chinese authorities agreed to permit teams of experts coordinated by the World Health Organization to visit China to contain the growing coronavirus outbreak. The news arrived as federal health officials announced expanded screening measures for passengers from China at 20 ports of entry to the United States. Other travel restrictions have been ruled out, officials said, though so far only five people in the United States were known to have been infected. Americans were then discouraged from traveling to any part of China.

Alex M. Azar II, the Secretary of Health and Human Services, at a news briefing in Washington, had reiterated the offer of scientific and logistical assistance and that he was "delighted" that China was accepting. The World Health Organization (W.H.O.) praised China's response to the outbreak, including its rapid identification of the virus and its "openness to sharing information with the W.H.O. and other countries." Even though the outbreak continued in China, federal officials maintained that the risk of infection remains low in the United States.

Dr. Robert Redfield, Director of the Centers for Disease and Control (CDC), said, "The coming days and weeks are likely to bring more cases, including the possibility of person-to-person spread. Our goal is to contain this virus and prevent the sustained spread of the virus in our country." Mr. Azar said, "This is a very fast-moving, constantly changing situation, Americans should know this is a potentially very serious public health threat, but at this point, Americans should not worry for their safety."

World Health Organization Emergency Chief said the few cases of human-to-human spread of the virus outside China, Japan, Germany, and Vietnam, were of "great concern" and were part of the reason the U.N. Health Agency's Director-General was receiving a committee of experts on January 30th to assess whether the outbreak should be declared a global emergency. The new virus has infected more people in China than were sickened there during the 2002-2003 SARS outbreak. More than a dozen nations as of January 30, 2020, have virus cases, including the United States, which are isolating patients and monitoring their contacts, as well as screening travelers from China and urging people to postpone trips there. But whether this virus can be contained depends on factors still unknown, like just how contagious it is and when in the course of the infection, the virus starts to spread.

Chapter 2

Is America Ready? "No Reason to Panic"

"We're definitely not ready. This virus can spread, and it can be deadly," said William Haseltine, infectious disease and drug development expert. President of the Global Health Think Tank Access Health International said a coast-to-coast outbreak is not unfathomable. "We've prepared for bioterrorism in general, but we haven't prepared for coronavirus as a potential threat specifically."

James Hodge, Professor of Law and Director of Arizona State University Center for Public Health Law and Policy, cautioned that although the coronavirus may not be more deadly than the common flu, there is no vaccine, known treatment, or cure. "Anytime we are dealing with an unknown condition that could strike and kill within a two-week period of time, that's serious, Hodge said. "We are seeing something that has gotten U.S. and international attention for good reasons."

Health and Human Services Secretary Alex Azar urged China to welcome a team of U.S. public health experts and scientists to gather necessary information about the virus. How long can a person be infected without showing symptoms? How does the virus spread? China reported that people without symptoms could spread the virus, but U.S. scientists were not convinced. "More cooperation and transparency are the most important steps you can take toward a more effective response," Azar said at a news conference on Tuesday, January 28th.

More than a dozen nations have contracted the virus, including the United States; they are isolating patients, monitoring their contacts, screening travelers from China, and urging people to postpone trips there. But whether this virus can be contained depends on factors still unknown, like how contagious it is and when in the course of the infection, the virus starts to spread. Countries, cities, and businesses across the globe in late January issued new travel warnings vastly expanding a cordon intended to control the flow of people to and from China, where the authorities were struggling to contain the outbreak of the new coronavirus. Officials at the United States Center for Disease Control and Prevention warned against non-essential travel to China, noting "limited access to adequate medical care in affected areas."

The World Health Organization revised its Global Risk Assessment for the outbreak from "moderate" to "high." However, it noted this shift in a footnote buried in a report published on January 27, 2020. The Global Risk Assessment coincided with a visit by the organization's Director-General, which confused the public about the severity of the outbreak, which has killed more than 100 people and has been seen in at least 14 countries. The World Health Organization was criticized after it refused twice in late January to declare a global emergency, despite its spread. The World Health Organization on January 30, 2020, announced the coronavirus outbreak a public health emergency of international concern as the person-to-person transmission of the virus was reported in the United States. The World Health Organization designator, pointing to an increase in the number of cases, indicated that international public health authorities now consider the respiratory virus a significant threat beyond China, where it originated in December.

In the U.S., a sixth person tested positive for the infection in the first case of human-to-human transmission. The U.S. Center for Disease Control and Prevention and state officials emphasized that the overall risk for people in the U.S. remains low. It is unknown what the future will bring to the United States, who appeared to impress on citizens that all is okay. Even though the U.S. was aware of China and a few cases in the U.S., the worst was yet to come. America was not ready, even when the state department told Americans not to travel to China, raising its travel alert to the highest on January 30, 2020. On January 28th, the U.S. Centers for Disease Control and Prevention advised travelers to avoid all non-essential trips to China. They issued a Level 3 warning for the country, citing the virus's spread and the lockdown of cities including Wuhan, which sits in the center of the outbreak.

The U.K. and New Zealand followed the U.S. in advising their citizens against non-essential travel to China. Some global companies have adjusted their operations in China. Starbucks Corp. said it had temporarily closed more than half its stores in the country due to the outbreak. Apple Inc. limited business travel to the country, closed retail stores, and limited store operating hours there. Other chains, including McDonald's Corp., closed stores in late January. United Airlines Holding Inc., on January 28, 2020, became the first U.S. carrier to cancel flights between the U.S. and China starting February 1st.

Fears in late January over the virus have hit U.S. based casinos operations. Las Vegas Sands Corp., Wynn Resorts Ltd., and MGM Resorts International have resorts in the region that generate 70% of people who travel to Macau, the only place in China where casinos are allowed.

Is America ready? With all the spread of the virus in China and other countries, including few limited cases in the United States. The pandemic virus that is growing and spreading is not being taken seriously by the United States. So, I guess, the United States only views the growth of the virus as "No reason to panic."

The World Health Organization on January 30, 2020, declared a global health emergency as the coronavirus outbreak spread well beyond China, where it emerged in December of 2019. The move reversed the organization's decision to hold off such a declaration. Since then, there have been thousands of new cases in China and clear evidence of human-to-human transmission in several other countries, including the United States. The declaration comes now because of fears that the coronavirus may reach countries with weak healthcare systems, where it could run amuck, potentially infecting millions of people and killing thousands.

The W.H.O. agency is governed by an annual convocation of the health ministers of all U.N. countries, and its role is only to offer advice. Governments then make their own decisions about how they protect themselves. Nonetheless, emergency declarations signal that the world's top health advisory body thinks the situation is grave. Many scientific experts welcomed the decision. The public health emergency "allows them to further lean into the role of global leadership for governments and the private sector," said Dr. Thomas R. Frieden, the former Director of the Centers for Disease Control and Prevention and a veteran of several global health emergencies. The first goal, he said, should be to understand how the virus is spreading, whether mostly in hospitals and clinics, what ages and sexes or professionals are most affected, how sick they become, and what risk factors are dangerous.

"W.H.O. is paralyzed for the same political reasons that ruined its scientific judgment in SARS, Ebola, and Zika," he said. "Borders are closed, aircraft grounded, and ships anchored as the W.H.O. mutely dithers over whether or not to declare an emergency." Experts at the W.H.O. have lavishly and repeatedly praised China's response as remarkably aggressive. China is building two hospitals, in just two weeks, to house coronavirus patients. Chinese scientists deposited the genetic signatures of the coronavirus in public databases, significantly speeding the development of diagnostic tests and potential vaccines.

The U.S. on Friday, January 31, 2020, imposed entry restrictions on foreign nationals and quarantines on Americans returning from the Chinese province at the center of the virus outbreak as markets tumbled over fears about the impact on global growth. Health and Human Services Secretary Alex Azar declared a public health emergency on January 31st over the coronavirus. He said foreign citizens who have traveled anywhere in China within the last 14 days would be denied U.S. entry, while Americans who visited Hubei province would be quarantined for up to two weeks. Simultaneously, Mr. Azar sought to minimize fears about the virus spreading further in the U.S. "I hope that people will see that their government is taking responsible steps to protect them," he said at a White House briefing. "The risk is low…but our job is to keep the risk low." Several confirmed cases in the U.S. as of late January, and the Centers for Disease Control and Prevention confirmed that 191 other people are being checked for possible infection. The number of people infected in China surpasses 9,700 as the death toll from the virus rose to 213.

The CDC called their quarantine move for 195 returning Americans as precautionary and preventative while describing the immediate risk to the general U.S. public as low. "If we take strong measures now, we may be able to blunt the impact of the virus on the U.S.," said Nancy Messonnier, Director of the National Center for Immunization and Respiratory Disease at the CDC. To counter the spread of the coronavirus outbreak, the Trump administration said on January 31st that it would bar entry by most foreign nationals who had recently visited China, putting some American travelers under a quarantine, as a rare public health emergency was declared. The temporary restrictions followed announcements by American Airlines, Delta Airlines, and United Airlines that they would suspend air service between the United States and China for several months. As of February 2nd, cases of the virus in China reached 17,205. The country's National Health Commission reported more than double the numbers afflicted worldwide nearly two decades ago by severe acute respiratory syndrome, or SARS. Deaths in China hit 361; the commission reported exceeding 349 deaths, which the World Health Organization declared in mainland China during the SARS crisis.

In the U.S., the Center for Disease Control and Prevention said a California resident was infected by a member of a person's household who became ill after returning from Wuhan, China, the epicenter of the outbreak. The transmission was the latest between two people in the U.S. after a Chicago woman who had traveled to Wuhan infected her husband following her return to the U.S. All other infected people in the U.S. had recently traveled to the Wuhan area. No U.S. deaths from the virus have been reported. The CDC added five confirmed coronavirus cases in the U.S. since its last update on February 2nd. Four occurred in California and the fifth in Massachusetts. CDC officials said Americans remain at low risk of infection. The CDC also said it expected the first week of February to receive approval from the Food and Drug Administration for a test developed to diagnose the infection. State and local health officials and health providers said they would test directly without sending samples to the CDC. U.S. National Security Advisor Robert O'Brian said February 2nd that the U.S. was prepared to send a CDC team to help but that Chinese officials hadn't responded.

Chapter 3

Coronavirus is Here to Stay, Affecting U.S. and China Businesses.

China's Communist Party leadership called the month-old coronavirus epidemic a "major test" on February 3rd. Other nations escalated efforts to isolate China, leading to unnerving China's stock market, depressing global oil prices, and raising anxiety about the world's populous country. The growing global movement to effectively cut off Chinas 1.4 billion people came as government officials reported that the new coronavirus strain had killed more in mainland China. 425 as of Tuesday, February 4th, more than the SARS outbreak in 2002-2003, confirming it as one of the deadliest epidemics in recent China history.

Many leading infectious disease experts say the outbreak is likely to become a pandemic, defined as a continuing epidemic on two or more continents, and that stringent anti-contagion restrictions may have come too late. "There is no sign that it's getting better," said Leo Poon, Division Head of the Public Health Laboratory Sciences Department at the University of Hong Kong. "We don't see a pattern of decline, and that is a problem." As of February 2nd, China had 20,438 cases, and more than 160 cases have been diagnosed in two dozen other countries, including 11 in the United States. During the SARS outbreak, China had 349 deaths and 5,327 cases, according to the World Health Organization. Government figures show that confirmed coronavirus infections are surging by more than 2,000 per day.

A patient diagnosed with the new coronavirus became Hong Kong's first fatality from the affliction on February 4th, as Thailand reported six more cases. Japan quarantined a cruise ship because of a passenger infection, and Macau shut its casinos, underscoring the contagious spread beyond China. Macau's casinos have struggled as the coronavirus outbreak has led to growing travel restrictions for visitors from the mainland. In further signs of the epidemic's disruptive effects, Britain and France advised all their citizens in mainland China to leave if they could. South Koreas Hyundai automaker idled factories because of China's supply chain problems. Within mainland China, the toll of the virus continued to climb fast, with 425 deaths and 20,438 confirmed cases as of February 2nd, Chinese health authorities reported, roughly double the figures four days earlier. By February 5th, the numbers in China had climbed to at least 490 dead and 24,324 confirmed cases. More than 180 infections have been confirmed in two dozen other countries and territories.

Of the patients that died in mainland China, more than 80% were older than 60, and more than 75% had an underlying health condition that put them at greater risk. With health officials scrambling to deal with an outbreak spreading worldwide, tour operations and travel agents in the New York area are bracing for the economic pain that will come with empty rooms in hotels and empty seats on the buses. Across the globe, cities are starting to experience the fallout from the precipitous drop in visitors from China. The Chinese government imposed a ban on organized tours, and many airlines have suspended flights to and from that country.

Health officials in New York had identified three possible cases of the virus. On February 4th, test results for one of the three patients, all of whom recently visited China, came back negative. The results for the other two patients were pending. The officials said the city was prepared for the viruses spread, but they cautioned people not to panic. In New York City, Chinese tourists represent the second-largest group of foreign travelers. Nationwide, China was the third-largest source of overseas visitors to the United States in 2018. Among cities, New York was the top destination, followed by Los Angeles.

A manager of China Tour Travel Services in Flushing, Queens, had booked hotel rooms and made sightseeing arrangements for 200 people, scheduled to arrive from China in the first two weeks of February, a typical number for early to mid-February. The manager, Bruce Zhu, said, "It's a big problem. We have to cancel the bookings and cancel the hotels. We lose a lot of money on bookings." He said he might have to lay off two of his five employees. Tourism Economics, in which travel industry research predicts a 28% drop in visitors to the United States from China in 2020 and $5.8 billion less in spending. The firm based its forecast on the timeline of the SARS outbreak in 2003, which lasted about four months, and the travel industry's rebound. It took another three years for the number of travelers from China to return to pre-SARS numbers.

The first week of February, before the Trump administration advised Americans not to travel to China, STR, a travel research company, said 2020 would be a "non-growth year" for the hotel industry's benchmark indicator. "There's never a good time for something like coronavirus," said Carter Wilson, STR's Senior Vice President of Consulting and Analytics, "but the U.S. hotel industry is in more of a vulnerable position now then it was three or four years ago."

In 2018, according to figures from NYC & Company, the city's Convention and Visitors Bureau, just under 8% of the foreign travelers who visited New York came from China. The number of Chinese visiting New York had surged since 2008 when officials from the United States and China cleared the way for vacationers to visit. For now, some restaurants and stores in Chinatown in

Manhattan are not seeing the usual crowds. Andy Wong, a manager at the Taiwan Pork Chop House on Doyers Street in Manhattan, said the crowds had become sparse since the outbreak of the coronavirus. Business is down at lunchtime when Wall Street types usually fill the tables, and tourism has dropped.

Still beyond a plunge in Chinese visitors, owners of the restaurants and stores in New York's three main Chinatowns, in lower Manhattan, Flushing, Queens, Sunset Park, and Brooklyn, the coronavirus and the fears it has stoked are hurting businesses. At restaurants in Manhattan's Chinatown, workers and owners said business had dropped 50-70% in the last ten days. Outside the office of Universal Vision in Flushing, which books sightseeing trips to Manhattan and places like Niagara Falls, brochures promised: "tours every day." But employees said there was no one to fill the seats on the company's minivans and buses. Sean F. Hennessey, an Assistant Professor at New York University who follows the travel industry, said the economic impact was likely to be greater than during the SARS outbreak. "New York will feel it," Mr. Hennessey said, referring to the effects of the coronavirus.

The pace of the new viral threat, which was reported on December 31, 2019, from Wuhan, China, is breathtaking: 28,353 cases and 565 deaths as of February 6th. The outbreak, which sees more cases reported by the hour, is primarily contained to mainland China: 265 cases have been reported elsewhere, including 12 in the United States and one death in Hong Kong and the Philippines. Government and public health officials are desperately trying to slow the spread of the respiratory virus with robust screening, quarantines, and travel bans. As infection disease specialists and scientists track the threats, they are studying past outbreaks to determine what the new coronavirus will do next.

A best-case scenario is containing the virus and eliminating it from human circulation. That is what happened in 2003 with another deadly virus, a severe acute respiratory syndrome known as SARS. But many researchers said 2019-NCoV might be here to stay, like Swine Flu, it could become a common ingredient in a winter soup of respiratory bugs that cause common colds and other illnesses-only without the fanfare of travel restrictions and global commerce disruption. It is very daunting to contain a respiratory virus, as we saw with H1N1. COVID-19 might establish itself as one of the community coronaviruses that we contend with for some time during the respiratory virus season.

Officials from the U.S. Centers for Disease Control and Prevention invoked the 2009 swine flu pandemic when discussing efforts to detect and contain the coronavirus. Agency officials would not speculate on when the outbreak might retreat. Nancy Messonnier, director of the CDC's National Center for Immunization and Respiratory Diseases, said a difference this time was the ability to prepare. "Rather than coming from abroad, that virus was on our doorstep when we recognized it," Messonnier said. "We are again seeing the emergence of a new virus that poses a very serious public health threat. This time, we do have time to prepare, and we have to prepare as if this were the next pandemic."

CDC officials predicted more cases in the United States, but they are working to slow the spread by expanding tests, isolating infected individuals, and restricting travel. "We have the opportunity to slow it down before it gets into the United States; we made an aggressive decision in front of an unprecedented threat. Action now had the biggest potential to slow this virus down." Experts suspect there are far more global cases than publicly reported. Last week in the first week of February, the University of Hong Kong estimated 75,815 had been infected in Wuhan as of January 25, 2020, and projected the epidemic would double every six days. The dire prediction included a caveat: little is known about the seasonality of the new coronavirus. It could be like the flu, which mainly circulates in the fall and winter. If it becomes a seasonal bug, infectious disease doctors say its spread could be limited during spring and summer months when respiratory viruses such as the flu or lesser-known coronaviruses fade because of heat and humidity.

Infectious disease doctors and scientists are gathering basic evidence about the coronavirus. They suspect the virus jumped from an animal to a human and can spread from human to human, but the unknown remains in late January and early February, including how deadly it is and if it can spread by infected people with no symptoms. Some experts were hopeful that China could get back to work Monday, the end of an extended holiday for workers in two dozen provinces. Such a move would signal the virus was beginning to be contained, but by the end of the day, that hope had failed. "Most pandemic experts believe it's no longer in the cards," said Stephen Morrison, Senior Vice President of Global Health Policy for the Center for Strategic and International Studies. "It is ripping through the country very rapidly." Morrison also said the lack of certainty has made it difficult for airlines and other businesses in China to plan.

The U.S. Chamber of Commerce said the most important thing was to contain the virus. "U.S. companies are taking responsible steps to address the threat and doing everything in their power to support relief efforts in China, the U.S. government is also meeting around the clock, and we trust that they are taking the appropriate steps to prioritize the safety and security of Americans."

Chapter 4

Remedies Being Sought for Virus

Desperate for a cure for the new coronavirus spreading quickly across the country, Chinese families are flocking online to seek experimental remedies that might be effective against the virus, despite government warnings that no proven treatments have been found. Among the most sought-after drugs is Kaletra, an antiretroviral for HIV made by U.S. pharmaceutical giant Abbvie Inc. that blocks the enzymes some viruses need to replicate. Relatives of Chen Ruoping joined a scramble for the drug, known in Mandarin as Kelizhi, after the 57-year old developed a fever and was diagnosed with a lung infection in January. Mr. Chen, who lives at the epicenter of the outbreak in the central city of Wuhan, was turned away at overrun hospitals that had run out of diagnostic kits for the coronavirus, pushing his son online for help. "Does anyone in Wuhan have Kelizhi?" the younger Mr. Chen wrote on China's Twitter-like Weibo social media platform. "I'm begging everyone; I will be responsible for all the consequences."

The World Health Organization on February 5th reported the largest single-day rise in new cases and said it was seeking $675 million in funding to help countries strengthen their public health capacities to prevent the viruses spread. The outbreak, as of the first week of February, has infected more than 24,000 people and killed at least 490, the most in Hubei province, of which Wuhan is the capital. The U.S. on February 5th evacuated a hundred more Americans from Wuhan, with two planes arriving at the Travis Air Force Base in Fairfield, California. Two more planes with passengers from Wuhan were expected in the U.S. on Thursday, February 6th.

Registry records show that researchers in China have applied more than ten drugs, including antimalarial chloroquine, HIV antiretroviral darunavir, and several flu medicines. Wuhan has designated about two dozen hospitals to treat the coronavirus and has rushed to build or repurpose several other facilities to treat the most severe cases. That still leaves thousands of confirmed and suspected patients in self-quarantine either at home or in the hotels with limited access to doctors. With the city's hospitals overcrowded and short on experimental drugs, some that suspect they might be infected are now taking their treatment into their own hands.

As the Wuhan outbreak picked up speed in late January, China's National Health Commission warned that no antiviral medications were effective, but suggested a mix of the antiretroviral drugs Lopinavir and Ritonavir, the same combination used in Kaletra. The next day, Wong Guangfa, a respiratory specialist at Peking University First Hospital, said he took the two drugs after becoming infected with the new virus while treating patients in Wuhan. "Many patients generally need more than a week or two weeks for their condition to improve," Dr. Wang told state media. His temperature began to drop within a day of taking the Kaletra mix, he said. Taking powerful medication without a doctor's supervision is dangerous, but the reports of Dr. Wang's success convinced the Chan family to risk it. Mr. Chan had recently undergone 12 rounds of chemotherapy for cancer.

The challenge was finding a drug. China's government typically supplies Kaletra only for HIV patients with a doctor's prescription. Chicago-based AbbVie said last month in January; they donated about $2 million worth of the drug as an "experimental option" in response to a request by Chinese authorities. But access was limited even inside Wuhan hospitals.

Chapter 5

No Word by Trump on Virus, Only Acquittal Victory Lap

With the coronavirus threatening the world and beginning to slowly filter into the United States, affecting thousands in China and killing hundreds, no word was mentioned by Trump about the pandemic that was spreading in low numbers in the United States. President Trump was delighting in his impeachment acquittal on February 6th, unleashing his fury against those who tried to remove him from office and pointing ahead to his re-election campaign. With the news of the coronavirus all over the media, there was not a solemn word by Trump about what was happening in China, which was the epicenter of the virus. There was no mention of possible things that the U.S. could do to help China fight the pandemic, which was growing and taking lives daily as the media was covering throughout the world. But all President Donald Trump could do was wave a newspaper front page that declared him "ACQUITTED." Trump denounced the impeachment proceeding as a "disgrace" and portrayed himself as a victim of political foes he labeled "scum," "sleaze bags," and "crooked" people. Trump unleashed broadsides that stunned the crowd at an annual bipartisan prayer breakfast. "It was evil, it was corrupt, it was dirty cops," Trump declared in a packed White House East Room, where he was surrounded by several hundred of his most loyal supporters.

"This should never happen to another president, ever." He conceded nothing regarding charges that he improperly withheld a White House meeting and military aid to pressure Ukraine to investigate Democratic rival, Joe Biden. "We went through hell, unfairly," Trump insisted. "Did nothing wrong." Venting for more than an hour, Trump ticked off names of the "vicious and mean" people he felt had wronged him: House Speaker Nancy Pelosi, Intelligence Committee Chairman Adam Schiff, and former FBI Director James Comey. He reveled in the verdict handed down by the GOP controlled Senate, saluting one-one in Oscar acceptance speech fashion the "Warrior" lawmakers who had backed him.

President Trump said, "We went through Russia, Russia, Russia," mocking the investigations into Moscow's interference in the 2016 presidential election on his behalf and ties between his campaign and Moscow. "It was all bullshit," he said, rare presidential use of profanity on camera in the East Room. Early on Thursday, February 6th, Trump shattered the usual veneer of bipartisanship at the National Prayer Breakfast in Washington by unleashing his fury against those who tried to impeach him; with Pelosi sitting on stage. "As everybody knows, my family, our great country, and your president have been put through a terrible ordeal by some very dishonest and corrupt people," Trump said at the annual event. "I don't like people who use their faith as justification for doing what they know is wrong," Trump said in an apparent reference to Utah Senator Mitt Romney, who cited his faith in becoming the only Republican to vote for Trump's removal. "Nor do I like people who say 'I pray for you' when you know that this is not so," he said, about Pelosi, who offered that message for the president when the two leaders have sparred publicly. Trump later said he "meant every word."

News of President Donald Trump's acquittal was seen across the world in all major newspapers. The question that must be asked: Where is the concern by Trump pertaining to the outbreak of the coronavirus in China? All the attention was focused on

President Donald Trump with minimal regard for the pandemic that has affected over 28,000 people and succumbed to 565 deaths as of February 6, 2020, moving aggressively to other countries, including the United States.

Now scientists are trying to figure out what must be done to end the global health emergency unleashed by the new coronavirus. As the outbreak accelerated and spreads, dozens of countries have deployed increasingly stringent measures to contain the epidemic. Almost as quickly, in a herculean effort, an international network of researchers at data and wet laboratories have started gathering and analyzing data to unmask and disarm this perplexing disease. In magnitude, scale, and velocity, this coronavirus is too big of a problem for any one team to solve. On February 11, 2020, China reported its most immense single-day death toll of 108, pushing the total reported dead worldwide beyond 1,000, with more than 42,600 people infected on four continents.

Let us start with what we know. The new coronavirus is a close cousin of viruses that infect bats. It jumped from an unconfirmed wild source (most likely bats) to an intermediate host, possibly pangolins or other small mammals, sold as food at a market in Wuhan, a transportation and commercial hub in central China. The infected people unknowingly spread it to others, setting off the deadly outbreaks journey. We now estimate that it takes five to six days-possibly upward of 14 days for someone to show symp-toms after becoming infected. For epidemiologists who track infec-tious diseases, the most pressing concerns are how to estimate the lethality of the disease and who is susceptible, getting detailed information on how it spreads; and evaluating the success of cen-tral measures so far. How much of it is hidden below the surface? Because the outbreak is still evolving, we cannot yet see the totality of those infected. Out of view is some proportion of mildly infected people, with minor symptoms or no symptoms, who no one knows is infected.

A fleet of invisible carriers sounds ominous, but in fact, an enormous hidden figure would mean fewer of the infected are dying. Usually, simple math would determine this "case fatality" ratio, dividing the total number of deaths by the total number of infected. In an emerging epidemic, however, both numbers keep changing, and sometimes at different speeds. This makes simple division impossible; you invariably get it wrong.

In 2003, during the early days of the SARS outbreak, the medical community got the math wrong. At first, we believed that case fatality hovered between 2% and 3%. It took two pages of longhand algebra, written in Oxford, England, coded into a computer in London, and then applied to data from Hong Kong, to get it right. The actual case fatality for Hong Kong was a staggering 17%. That is not to suggest we are facing as dire a scenario now. Several groups use their own methods to calculate a preliminary estimate of the new viruses' lethality.

Knowing the number of people likely to die, or who get seriously sick, or have zero symptoms, will help health authorities determine the strength of the response required. They can better estimate how many isolation beds, heart, and lung machines, among other things that are needed. In January, to start understanding the severity of the illness, Chinese experts began analyzing the initial 425 confirmed cases of infection. It was found that 65% of people had neither visited a market nor been exposed to another person showing pneumonia-like symptoms, which implied the possibility that some infected people do not suffer from obvious symptoms-meaning the illness isn't always severe.

Along with getting a group on the level of severity is figuring out susceptibility or who is most at risk for infection. The data so far indicates that this would include older adults, the obese, and people with underlying medical conditions. There are few reports of children becoming infected. But are they not showing symptoms, or are they immune? Could they infect others as silent carriers? A study must be made for those under 18 to find out; the answers could help us fine-tune public health measures. For example, should schools in China and Hong Kong remain closed? We must also refine what we know about how the new coronavirus is passed between people. Even as the outbreak appears to keep escalating, we believe the rapid-sometimes necessarily draconian-response of governments and health authorities has made a dent in transmission. In another recent study, it was estimated how many people could get infected if there were no drastic public health interventions. The goal was to sound the alarm over what could be so that it would not be.

Scientists are working towards quantifying the effectiveness of the response. We need to find out if the virus's basic reproductive numbers have dropped. While earliest estimates showed that typically every person infected by the new coronavirus passes it to 2-2.5 others, it is still too early to know if measures have reduced the number to below the critical threshold of 1. Simultaneously the World Health Organization is closely watching the rest of the world for any large, sustained outbreaks that might resemble ground zero in Wuhan. The W.H.O. expects more clarity within days or weeks. On Monday, February 10th, the largest concentration of infected patients in a single location outside mainland China, at more than 130 people, was on a cruise ship, the Diamond Princess, which quarantined at Japans Yokohama port.

Scientists need to appraise the control or social distancing measures deployed since the outbreak began. The challenge involves quantifying how many infections were prevented through measures such as social distancing, wearing masks, closing schools, and locking down cities. One possible approach to this assessment in China could involve using location services data from cell phones. As the World Health Organization determines research priorities from their headquarters in Geneva, the hope is that the science being urgently coordinated will also fight the crisis on all fronts. It could help battle emerging "infodemic," the cacophony of real news, fake news, and pseudoscience that feed uncertainty and breed panic. It could help roll back some measures seemingly fueled by populism and nativism. The travel advisories, outright travel bans, immigration controls, and xenophobic treatment of people from different places are doing significant harm.

The goal is to stay at least a couple of steps ahead of the epidemic curve. Scientists must prepare health authorities to catch any subsequent waves of infection and prepare for the possibility that the virus could appear seasonally. Maybe one day, it could be only as bad as the common cold. The W.H.O. epidemiologists had seen record-breaking outbreaks before and witnessed the world rally. If we all play our roles and remain on guard, then chances are we will defeat the new coronavirus too.

Now Mr. Trump confronts another epidemic in the form of the coronavirus, this time at the head of the country's health care and national security agencies. The illness has infected few people in the United States, but health officials fear it could soon spread more widely. While Mr. Trump has kept his distance from the issue, public health experts worry that his extreme fear of germs, disdain for scientific and bureaucratic expertise, and suspicion of foreigners could be a dangerous mix. "Having a head of state who is trusted, who has a credible message delivered, consistent in communication and consistent with the evidence, is absolutely necessary," said Dr. Jennifer Nuzzo, a Senior Scholar at the Johns Hopkins Center for Health Security. "There's so much misinformation out there, so a central role is for a leader to be a go-to source for credible information.

For the most part, Mr. Trump has been uncharacteristically restrained in his commentary about the virus, delegating the response to senior health officials. At the end of January, Mr. Trump created a 12-member coronavirus task force, managed by the National Security Council. It includes the of Health and Health and Human Services Secretary, Alex M. Azar II; Dr. Anthony S. Fauci, the

Director of the National Institute of Allergy and Infectious Diseases at the National Institute of Health, and Dr. Robert R. Redfield, the Director of the Centers for Disease Control and Prevention. All three have experience dealing with infectious diseases, especially Mr. Fauci, who has helped manage the response to numerous outbreaks, including the AIDS epidemic, the SARS virus, and Ebola.

Speaking to a meeting of the nation's governors on February 10th, Trump predicted that the virus would have run its course by spring and again referred to the Chinese president. "The virus that we are talking about having to do, a lot of people think that it goes away in April, with the heat, as the heat comes in, typically that will go away in April," Mr. Trump said. Referring to the United States, he added: "We're in great shape. We have 12 cases, 11 cases, and many of them are in good shape now." Public health experts questioned the speculative nature of his comments. "I think there is a lot we don't know about this virus, and I'm not quite sure we can say definitely that it will dissipate with warmer weather," said Dr. Katz, Director of the Center for Global Health Science and Security at Georgetown University. "Relying on the fact that it's going to warm up in April as a reassurance that the virus will be controlled by then I think is arguable," added Dr. James M. Hugh's, a Professor Emeritus of Medicine at Emery University.

Other comments from Mr. Trump about the disease have been inaccurate or met with criticism. In late January, he wrote on Twitter that five coronavirus cases had been confirmed in the United States just hours after a sixth had been confirmed. Addressing the virus on February 2nd, Mr. Trump boasted on Fox News, "We pretty much shut it down," apparently referring to an executive order the president had issued two days earlier, barring entry to the United States by foreign citizens who traveled to China in the past two weeks. Some health experts worry that Mr. Trump over-promised because the order, which the White House announced abruptly with little outside consultation, is unlikely to prevent the illness from reaching the United States. Federal health officials say they assume the number of cases in the United States is likely to increase.

"Trump has the right people, but the wrong instincts, and the wrong structure," said Ronald Klain, who directed the Obama administration's response to the 2014 Ebola crisis. "Our government is staffed with the best experts, scientists, and medical leaders in the world. But Trump's instincts, anti-science, anti-expert, isolationist, and xenophobic risk will eschew that advice at critical points. "Another factor is Mr. Trump's lifelong obsession with personal hygiene. While he has shown little interest in health or science policy, he has often spoken of his extreme revulsion to germs. As a result, Mr. Trump generally avoids the political tradition of shaking dozens of hands after his speeches and rallies, and frequently uses hand sanitizer. He is quick to banish aides who cough and sneeze in his presence.

Chapter 6

World Health Organization Asks for Help as Virus Increases in China

Japanese health officials stated on Thursday, February 6th, that ten more people were sickened with the virus aboard one of two quarantined cruise ships with 5,400 passengers and crew. China then reported 73 more deaths; because of this, the World Health Organization appealed for more funds to help countries battle the spread of the disease. The ships in Japan and Hong Kong are caught up in a global health emergency that worsens by the day. In the port of Yokohama, just outside Tokyo, health workers said ten more people from the Diamond Princess were confirmed ill with the virus, in addition to 10 others who tested positive on Wednesday, February 5th.

The latest infections included four Japanese, two Americans, two Canadians, one New Zealander, and one Taiwanese. Most were in their 60's and 70's. They were dropped off as the ship docked and transferred to nearby hospitals for further tests and treatment. The 3,700 people on board faced a two-week quarantine in their cabins. More tests are pending on 171 others who had symptoms or had contact with a man diagnosed with the virus after leaving the ship in Hong Kong. The ships are caught up in a global health emergency that seems to worsen by the day. On Thursday, February

6th, the number of confirmed cases jumped by 3,694 to 28,018, and the death toll rose to 565 deaths.

The Director-General of the World Health Organization, Tedros Adhanom Ghebreyesus, asked for $675 million to help countries address the expected spread of the virus. He acknowledged that the sum is a lot but told a news briefing that "it's much less than the bill we will face if we do not invest in preparedness now." Tedros said that in the last 24 hours, the U.N. health agency had seen the most significant jump in cases since the start of the epidemic. China has vigorously defended its epidemic control measures and called on other nations not to go overboard in their responses.

Chinese authorities strengthened their coronavirus lockdown Thursday, February 6th, in a desperate move to contain the deadly scourge of infections. They ordered house-to-house searches rounding up the sick and warehousing them in a convention center, and other buildings converted into makeshift quarantine internment camps. The steps were announced by the top official leading the response to the outbreak as she visited the central Chinese city of Wuhan, the epicenter of the epidemic. Government figures on February 7th showed the virus had killed at least 636 people and infected at least 31,161, and many believe those official statistics are far from being complete.

Authorities have begun to direct patients in Wuhan to makeshift hospitals intended to house thousands of people. It was unclear whether the new shelters were equipped or staffed to provide even primary care to patients and protect against spreading the virus. "This is almost a humanitarian disaster because there are not sufficient medical supplies, "said Willy Wo-Lap Lam, an adjunct professor at the Center for China Studies at the Chinese University of Hong Kong.

New cases of the coronavirus rose sharply after Chinese authorities changed the criteria for diagnosing the illness, raising questions about how soon the outbreak will peak. On February 13th, health officials of Hubei province, the epicenter of the infections, announced the largest one-day jump in cases 14,890 on Wednesday, February 12th, about nine times the number of new cases a day earlier. Epidemiologists, government officials, and investors might need to recalibrate their projections for a virus that is not understood.

Investors had pushed U.S. stocks to records as Chinese officials touted gains in the fight against the fast-spreading illness that has gripped central China for the past month, fixing their attention on one number, a drop in the growth rate of new infections. The vast majority of February 13th newly confirmed cases-13,332-were retroactively reclassified. But the broader classification rules mean the daily rise in the number of new cases could continue to grow because more undiagnosed cases come to light. Goldman Sachs Group Inc., pointing to the virus figures, told clients in a note on Wednesday, February 13th, "the spread of the virus has slowed, as the number of new cases nationwide has gradually declined." Shortly after, the U.S. stock market opened with the Dow Jones industrials going up.

Authorities do not yet have an accurate estimate of the number of infected people in Wuhan. Mr. Chan, a top law enforcement official from Beijing, helping oversee the crisis in Wuhan, added that "the base number of potentially infected in Wuhan may still be relatively large." Still, the outbreak could be more severe than figures suggest. Unlike Hubei, other parts of China require either gene sequencing or lab test to confirm the pathogen, meaning not all cases may be being detected and tallied. In a document circulated to hospitals across China last week, the National Health Commission updated its case categories for Hubei to separate clinically diagnosed cases from suspected cases. Hubei patients whose chest scans showed signs of pneumonia would be included in this category, while those whose chest scans did not would remain as suspected cases.

Hubei's Health Commission said the goal was to let more patients be treated as confirmed cases so that more could be cured. Officials spent the past few days combing through suspected instances to identify the thousands of cases added to the province's confirmed tally on Thursday, February 13th, which now stands more than 48,000 cases. At the same time, Hubei began blanket screening using the looser diagnostic standards, picking up patients with fevers whose chest scans showed lung infections, and sending them to designated hospitals. Only 20% to 30% of all pneumonia cases can be proven in testing to be linked to any pathogen, Tang Zhaouhui, a respiratory disease doctor from Beijing Chaoyang Hospital.

In Beijing, Chinese authorities saw another jump in infections identifying 5,090 new coronavirus cases. A recent increase in their daily total has stirred concerns about the trajectory of the disease. It has raised fresh worries over whether China is offering an accurate appraisal of the epidemic scope. On Thursday and Friday, February 13th and 14th alone, China confirmed cases to its official count, bringing the total number of patients infected by the coronavirus to more than 63,000 people as of Thursday the 13th of February.

Chinese President Xi Jinping on February 14th pledged to improve China's epidemic-prevention and public-health systems, according to state-run China Central Television. "We must fix shortcomings, plug loopholes, and strengthen weak links," Mr. Xi said. In a sign that China remains far from resuming everyday life after lockdowns that have shut down businesses across the country for weeks, Beijing's municipal government said February 14th that people who return to the capital after traveling outside of the city must stay at home for 14 days.

The increase in cases came after authorities in Hubei province, the epicenter of the outbreak, changed how they diagnosed patients. They previously had relied on lab tests, which scientists said took too long to conduct and could be unreliable. Now, beginning with a February 13th tally report, Hubei counts patients whose corona-virus infections are confirmed by X-rays of lungs or other means used to diagnose patients clinically. Chinese President Xi Jinping assured counterparts that his government is sparing no effort in a "people war" against an epidemic that has killed more than 1,380 individuals. His foreign minister has worked the phones during the past few weeks of February, relaying a message of calm and confidence to counterparts and senior officials from more than 20 countries. "There is still considerable uncertainty about the number of possible cases and the mortality rate of the virus," said Ryan Manuel, Manager Director of a Hong Kong based research firm and an expert on the country's public health system.

Chapter 7

Chinese Search for Adequate Protection as Beijing's own People Fight Coronavirus

Chinese medical workers at the forefront of the fight against the coronavirus epidemic are often becoming victims, partly because of government missteps and logistical hurdles. After the virus emerged in Wuhan late last year of 2019, city leaders played down its risks, so doctors didn't take precautions. When the outbreak could no longer be ignored, officials imposed a lockdown on Wuhan that expanded across the surrounding Hubei province and then swaths of China. The last travel cordons may have shown the epidemic and slowed deliveries into Hubei, leaving medical workers short on protective wear. On Friday, the 14th of February, the Chinese government, for the first time, disclosed the toll the outbreak that was taking on hospital employees: 1,216 medical workers had contracted the virus, and six had died.

Chinese president and Communist Party leader, Xi Jinping, has praised hospital workers in Hubei as heroes and mobilized the country in a "peoples war" against the coronavirus. But hospital workers in Wuhan said they often felt frustrated and alone. Some have scrambled to buy protective gear with their own money, begged from friends, or relied on donations from other parts of China and abroad. Others have avoided eating and drinking for long stretches because they would have to discard safety gowns that were not replaceable. Younger staff were assigned to more critical cases, with the expectation that if they got sick, they would be more likely to recover.

Even as Chinese officials disclosed how many medical workers had been sickened and killed by the virus, key questions remain, experts said, including how the workers became infected and whether the rate of transmission was slowing. Such omissions could make it more difficult for other countries to assess and their own risks. "Clearly, it would have been useful for other parts of China who are beginning to struggle with this outbreak as well as for the rest of the world to have this type of data as soon as possible," said Malik Peiris, a virologist at the University of Hong Kong. Dr. Tedros Adhanam Ghebreyesus, Director of The World Health Organization, said it is seeking more information about the time period and circumstances surrounding the infections of health care workers. "This is a critical piece of information because health care workers are the glue that holds the health system and outbreak response together," Dr. Tedros said.

Doctors and other hospital workers have also come under pressure not to speak out. But many do out of desperation. "For the first time, I felt helpless confronting the system," Chang Le, a doctor at Hankou Hospital in Wuhan, said in an online message pleading for more medical masks. His plea was deleted by the censors. "It's only today that I've grasped just how hard it is for us front-line medical workers." The Chinese government has acknowledged problems in medical supplies for Hubei and repeatedly promised to accelerate deliveries. Strains in medical supplies may have been unavoidable as the virus spreads at a pace that seemed to catch the government off guard. But the sweeping restrictions across China to contain the virus also slowed production and delivery of much-needed medical equipment, said doctors, factory managers, and aid workers.

With medical supplies so scarce, many health care workers in Wuhan also said they had to accept substandard gowns, gloves, and masks. Outside the Wuhan Fourth Hospital, medical workers waited near a truck as a delivery man in a full-body medical suit handed down boxes of masks and gowns. One hospital worker explained that the gowns were not of a high enough grade to withstand a viral contagion. "But this is all we could get," she said, "we just have to accept what they send us." Life has become a scramble; many said: treating patients for much of the day: hunting for protective gear for the rest. The shortage has forced employees, like Dr. Chang, from the city's hospitals to appeal for donations of N95 masks, a type of respirator best suited to guarding against viruses-and other personal protective equipment on Chinese social media sites.

Dr. Peng Zhiyong, 53, head of the department of critical care medicine at Wuhan University's Zhongnan Hospital, said in an interview in early February that his team was running dangerously low on full-body medical suits and masks. "We can only get one break during the day," he said. "Just one, to drink water and eat. Because if you leave, you don't have any new suits to get back into." In a furious social media post, Dr. Chang, the doctor at the Hankou Hospital, described his experience trying to get 10,000 N95 respirator masks from the Red Cross. He was eventually given more than 9,000 masks of inferior quality, he said. "I just wanted to cry," he said at the end of is video message.

Just a week later, China's Politburo Standing Committee, the Communist Party's topmost council, said problems with insufficient beds, medical personnel, and other medical resources persisted across Hubei. According to official data from the province, deliveries of high-quality masks and other items have accelerated. Health workers in China generally have been following W.H.O.'s guidelines to use so-called "standard precautions," which included surgical masks rather than more expensive N95 masks to cover their mouths and noses. The Center for Disease Control and Prevention, on the other hand, has instructed health care providers to use N95's, which block out much smaller particles than surgical masks do.

Big Chinese corporations and wealthy individuals have been donating, many generously to help the pandemic that has hit the country with 1.4 billion people. But they also try to keep low profiles for fear of offending a government that is eager to take credit for any success and quick to suspect outside groups of challenging it. It is evident on the front lines of the outbreak, where workers have lacked the proper equipment to keep themselves safe. Doctors and nurses wear disposable raincoats instead of protective gowns. They wear ordinary and inadequate surgical masks while conducting dangerous throat swab tests. They wear adult diapers because, once they take off their one-piece protective suits, the suits will have to be thrown away. They get only one per day. The authorities said on February 17th that over 3,000 medical workers had been infected though not all got the virus from work.

Ordinary Chinese people have set up social media groups to help patients find hospital beds, get volunteers to drive them to hospitals, and scavenge the world for protective gear. In coordination with the government, they could do much more. "We're just a small boat with limited capacity," said Ponda Yin, a designer in Beijing who organized a We Chat volunteer group of about 200 people to help find protective supplies for front line medical workers.

The Red Cross Society is notorious for corruption and inefficiency. The Chinese news media had reported on many of its scandals, including one nine years ago, when a person who reportedly held a senior position shared pictures of her opulent lifestyle online. The Red Cross Society has been slow in giving away masks and other supplies according to an analysis by people in China based on incomplete data. When the society did give out masks, it gave the best and the most directly to local government agencies instead of frontline hospitals.

On February 11th, the Wuhan government's epidemic-fighting central command, which counts top city officials among its members, received nearly 19,000 N95 medical masks, considered among the most effective in filtering particles. Union Hospital, one of Wuhan's most prominent public hospitals, received only 450. It was only one of four hospitals that received masks. On February 20th, all N95 masks went to local health commissions. None went to hospitals. If the Red Cross Society is a bottleneck in distributing medical supplies, the local and central government can sometimes become obstacles in private efforts to make, buy, and distribute these supplies. The Communist Party does not trust the country's businesses. In Xiantao, a city 70 miles from Wuhan and one of the world's biggest manufacturing centers for protective supplies, the local government shut down all but 10 of its protective gear factories on February 3rd.

A local official told the official People's Daily newspaper last week that the city had made the decision for quality control reasons. Out of 113 sizeable companies in the city, only two have the certificates to sell protective medical gowns in China. The majority of Xiantao's non-woven fabric products are for export only. Nonsense, said a factory owner in Xiantao who asked to be identified by his surname, Wong, for fear of retribution. The protective suits he makes for his British and American clients must meet standards that are equal to, if not higher than, those of China anyway. The real reason that Xiantao officials do not want to be held responsible is if factory workers become infected or if quality problems emerge. Two other factory owners who requested anonymity for fear of reprisals and a contention backed by local media reports in China agreed that in this extraordinary time, the government should set prices and scrutinize quality closely. Local officials said that the city allowed 73 more companies to go back to work by February 9th. But most of the factories remain idle, Mr. Wong and others said.

Xiantao officials blocked volunteers from Jingzhou, a city in Hubei 100 miles to the west, from getting the supplies it needs. Xiantao authorities tried to confiscate their gear at a checkpoint as they were leaving, and they were kicked out of the city. The volunteer asked to be recognized by the surname Zhang because he is not authorized to speak to the news media. Mr. Zhang said he and other volunteers had to step in because the Jinzhou Health Commission was overwhelmed and too bureaucratic to move fast enough to provide supplies to local hospitals. Photos and videos he shared on social media showed that volunteers had delivered protective clothing, goggles, and medical alcohol to hospitals. "I almost cried," he told a chat group when he saw that doctors and nurses at a local fever clinic had nothing for protection except ordinary surgical masks. The head of the clinic was so grateful; he said that she gave him four watermelons.

Volunteers like Mr. Zhang raise money for supplies through social media. One of his chat groups is made mostly of entrepreneurs like Mr. Leu, a tech entrepreneur in his 50's who wanted only his surname used for fear of retribution. The business owners in Mr. Liu's group have experience dealing with government. Some of them are wary of stepping on the toes of the public health authorities, who can go after them for any potential violation of public fundraising rules. If they must stay clear of a murky line, Mr. Liu argued, they probably will not be able to do anything. "Human lives should come above everything else," Mr. Liu said. Is it possible that this same attitude could be followed throughout the world, including the United States?

Chapter 8

Virus Causes Severe Disruption in U.S., but White House Dismisses Concerns

The nation would see 'severe' disruption to daily life; a top federal health official warned on February 25th that the deadly coronavirus could cause 'severe' disruptions in the United States as global experts struggle to fend off the outbreak and avoid a pandemic. "Disruption to everyday life may be severe," Nancy Messonnier, Director of the Center for Disease Control and Prevention, National Center for Immunization and Respiratory Diseases, warned at a news conference on February 25th. Schools could be closed, mass public gatherings suspended, and businesses forced to have employees work remotely, she said. Messonnier said the coronavirus has caused sickness and death and sustained person to person transmission, two of the three factors for a pandemic. "As community spread is detected in more and more countries, the world moves closer to meeting the third criteria, the worldwide spread of the new virus," Messonnier said.

Although the World Health Organization determined on February 24th that the term pandemic "did not fit the facts," experts said it very soon could. Dennis Carroll, former Director of the U.S. Agency for International Development's Global Health Security and Development Unit, credited China's "extraordinary control measures" with delaying the spread of the virus. Avoiding the pandemic is "very unlikely, the dramatic uptick of cases in South Korea, Iran, and Italy are reflective of a self-sustaining spread of the virus and a clear message that the horse is out of the barn," Carroll said to the news media on February 25th.

Melissa Nolan, a medical doctor and professor of epidemiology at the University of South Carolina's Arnold School of Public Health, cited new clusters in Iran, which faces at least 95 cases and has had 16 deaths, and Italy, which is dealing with 322 cases. "If we continue to see focalized local transmission in areas outside of China, the W.H.O. will need to reconvene," Nolan said on February 25th. "We are very close to seeing this virus becoming a pandemic," Nolan said; responses to the outbreaks in Iran and Italy could help health officials in other countries prepare their own medical and quarantine policies before an outbreak. That is crucial, said Robert Glatter, an Emergency Physician at New York's Lenox Hill Hospital who fears the world in on the "cusp" of a pandemic. "Trying to contain a disease which spreads like influenza, in this case, COVID-19, is almost impossible," he said. "We are talking about rapid-fire and sustained transmission." That means redirecting the focus from containment measures to preparing to treat significant numbers of sick patients with antivirals while continuing the effort to develop a vaccine. Beyond an epidemic, which involves a defined region, a pandemic has a global impact. It can be a moving target; there is no threshold, such as the number of deaths or infections.

W.H.O., which could make a pandemic declaration, describes a pandemic as "an epidemic occurring worldwide, or over a very widespread area, crossing international boundaries and usually affecting a large number of people." W.H.O. Director-General Tedros Adhanom Ghebreyesus does not want to go there. "I have spoken consistently about the need for facts, not fears," Tedros said. "Using the word 'pandemic' now does not fit the facts, but it may undoubtedly cause fear. Ogbonnaya Omenka, an Assistant

Professor and Public Health Specialist at Butler University's College of Pharmacy and Health Sciences, said he understands the concerns. The main implication of declaring a pandemic is requiring, or at least further urging, national governments to prepare facilities and health workers to treat a lot of patients; he told the news media, "Not only is this costly, but it may also trigger panic," he warned. "Countries may as well put in place these plans without the official announcement," Tedros stressed that a pandemic declaration would not eliminate the need for health authorities to continue testing, limiting contact with the sick and encouraging frequent handwashing-the front-line defense. Tedros noted that cases in China had declined for the past three weeks in Wuhan, where health services were stretched when the outbreak began in December, the fatality rate is 2%-4%. Elsewhere in China, its less than 1%.

This season's flu death rate in the USA is less than 0.1%, according to the CDC. More than 30 million Americans have suffered from the flu this season, while the global number of confirmed coronavirus cases has reached 100,000. There is a vaccine for the flu. Labs around the world are scrambling to develop one for the coronavirus. President Donald Trump requested $2.5 billion to fight the virus, including more than $1 billion in developing a vaccine. At a news conference on February 25th in India, Trump tried to tamp down concerns, saying the virus was "Very well under control in our country," confirmed cases totaled 57 on February 25th. No one has died in the USA, although one American died in Wuhan. "We have very few people with it, and…the people are all getting better," Trump said.

Messonnier acknowledged the CDC struck a more urgent tune in warnings about the virus in the USA. The proliferation of coronavirus in countries outside China raised the agency's expectations that the virus will spread here. "People are concerned about the situation-I would say rightfully so," she said. "But we are putting our concerns to work preparing. Now is the time for businesses, hospitals, communities, schools, and everyday people to begin preparing as well."Trump administration health officials urged the public on February 25th to prepare for the "inevitable" spread of the coronavirus within the U.S., escalating warnings about a growing threat from the virus to Americans' everyday lives. The warnings from officials with the Centers for Disease Control and Prevention, the National Institute of Health, and other agencies contrasted sharply with assessments from President Donald Trump and other White House officials, who have largely dismissed concerns about the virus. The mixed messages continued on Tuesday, February 25th, as dire warnings issued to senators and the media early in the day gave way to a more positive assessment, after the Dow Jones industrial average plunged 3.4%, bringing a two-day loss to 1,900 points, the biggest in two years.

"We believe the immediate risk here in the United States remains low and were working hard to keep the risk low," Anne Schuchat, the CDC's Principal Deputy Director, said during a convened afternoon media briefing. Earlier in the day, CDC officials and others sounded a more pressing alarm. "Ultimately, we expect we will see community spread in the United States. It's not a question of if this will happen, but when this will happen, and how many people in the country will have a severe illness," said Nancy Messonnier, Director of the National Center for Immunization and Respiratory Diseases at the CDC, during a morning briefing with reporters. Messonnier noted the rapid surge in cases in new locations outside mainland China in the past several days prompted the change in official warnings.

There is growing evidence that efforts to contain the spread of the virus outside of China have failed. There are now almost 1,000 cases in South Korea, at least 15 people have died in Iran, and new cases were reported for the first time in Switzerland, Austria, and at a luxury resort in Spain. In the United States, there are now 57 people with the virus, all but 14 of them are evacuees from the Diamond Princess cruise ship. Messonnier noted the spread of the new cases without a known source of exposure in multiple nations. Evidence of what's called "community spread," she said, is triggering new strategies to confront the respiratory virus, including urging businesses, health-care facilities, and even schools to plan now for ways to limit the impact of the illness where it spreads in the community.

Health leaders voiced similar warnings in a closed-door briefing February 25th for senators. Senator Patty Murray said officials had cautioned them that there was a "very strong chance of an extremely serious outbreak of the coronavirus here in the United States." At this point, it was, whom to believe? Not long after that, though, National Economic Council Director Larry Kudlow went on TV to try to assure concerns over the coronavirus and its impact on the U.S. economy, saying, "We have contained this. I won't say it's alright, but it's pretty close to alright," Kudlow told CNBC's Kelly Evans on "The Exchange. "Even top GOP lawmakers struggled to explain the inconsistent messages coming from the administration. "I can't comment on what the White House has been saying on this, because the people who work for the White House are not saying that," said Senator Roy Blunt, R-Mo.

The chaotic messaging threatened to obscure urgent public health advice coming from the CDC early on Tuesday, February 25th, when officials said the agency would be focusing on containing the spread of the virus in the United States, as well as warning people to prepare. "Disruptions to everyday life may be severe, but people might want to start thinking about now," said Messonnier, a top CDC health official. She said parents might want to call their local school offices to see what kinds of plans they have in place and consider options for childcare. Businesses need to consider replacing in-person meetings with telework, Messonnier said. Schools should consider ways to limit face to face contacts, such as dividing students into smaller groups, internet-based learning, or even closing schools. Local officials should consider modifying, postponing, or canceling large gatherings. Hospitals should consider ways to triage patients that do not need urgent care and recommend patients delay surgery that isn't absolutely necessary.

Some senators who attended the February 25th closed-door briefing downplayed any alarmist tone from the health officials. However, Senator Lamar Alexander, R-Tenn., said senators were told the number of cases in the United States would inevitably grow. "What we heard was that it's inevitable that we'll have more than 14 cases as time goes on," Alexander said. "And what we'll try to do is the same thing we've already done through quarantining and monitoring through our public health system to limit that as much as possible." Senator John Neely Kennedy, R-La., criticized the lawmakers briefing because he said that while issuing dire warnings, officials could not answer his basic questions. "I thought a lot of the briefing was bullshit," Kennedy said. "They would answer the question but dodge, bob, and weave. I understand there is a lot they do not know. I get that. But they need to answer the questions straight up." Blunt, Kennedy, and Senator Mitt Romney, R-Utah, were among the GOP senators who told health officials about concerns during the closed-door briefing, including the level of spending the administration is prepared to commit, the adequacy of preparations, and the length of time for the development of a vaccine.

During a crisis, presidents are looked to for direct and honest assessments of threats and reassurance to the public about their impact. During the swine flu outbreak of 1976, President Gerald R. Ford announced during a news conference that the government planned to vaccinate "every man, woman, and child in the United States." Mr. Ford himself was photographed receiving the vaccine in the White House as part of a public awareness campaign. Responding to the Ebola outbreak in West Africa in 2014,

President Barack Obama visited the Centers for Disease Control and Prevention in Atlanta to announce a new military command in Liberia with 3,000 doctors and other personnel.

Mr. Trump, in contrast, contradicted his own health experts in a news conference on Wednesday, February 26th, insisting that the spread of the virus was not inevitable, and ended up excoriating tow of his favorite foils Speaker Nancy Pelosi and Senator Chuck Schumer, the minority leads, for "trying to create a panic." For three and a half years, Mr. Trump has repeatedly proved an unreliable narrator on various subjects. At times, he has exaggerated threats, like talking up the caravans of migrants he claimed were storming the southern border before the 2018 midterm elections. Other times, he has minimized potentially serious dangers that could be politically damaging, like the renewed nuclear threat posed by North Korea after the failure of his talks with its leader, Kim Jong-Un, and now, the global spread of the coronavirus, which he has persistently tried to play down.

In his response to the coronavirus, Mr. Trump has made two inaccurate or questionable claims; misstating the number of Americans infected by the virus and claiming repeatedly it "miraculously goes away" when warmer spring weather arrives. A prediction that health experts have said is premature. Mr. Trump based that prediction on a comment made at one of his briefings when an expert noted that temperatures could affect the spread of viruses. Mr. Trump has used that data point as evidence for his repeated insistence made in public and private to guest at his Mar-a-Lago resort in Palm Beach, Fl, that the global outbreak will all be behind him by April. The president, as he often does, has also focused on the coverage of his response, complaining that he is being mistreated and blaming the news media. "If the virus disappeared tomorrow, they would say we did a really poor and incompetent job," he tweeted on February 25th. "Not fair, but it is what it is. So far, by the way, we have not had one death. Let's keep it that way."

Trump's allies said the fact that the president chose to address the growing public health crisis quickly after returning from a trip to India showed how seriously he was taking the outbreak. But privately, they say he has been reluctant to give in to what he has called an "alarmist" view's potential to cause damage as he warily watches the effect of the outbreak on the stock market. He has been rattled by the Wall Street reaction to the spread of the virus in places like Italy, lashing out at the news media in tweets and accusing journalists of intentionally trying to harm the stock market.

As Ebola presented both a health and political threat to his administration in 2014, Mr. Obama carefully hewed to proven science, which he repeatedly invoked in his carefully calibrated public messages. "We have to be guided by science. We have to remember the basic facts," he said in an October 2014 radio message. Mr. Trump, in contrast, has not been focused on scientific detail. The Secretary of Health and Human Services, Alex M. Azar II, has told officials they should give the notoriously impatient president simple, paint by numbers briefings on coronavirus. But an immense fear among experts in the field has been that he would contradict scientific experts. "That's where Trump is most pernicious, potentially," said Ron Klain, who served as Mr. Obama's "Ebola Czar," and now is an advisor to the presidential campaign of former Vice President Joseph R. Biden Jr.

As Mr. Trump faces the first public health emergency of his presidency, his go-to pattern of making false claims could also prove harder to sell to the public. "When you're trying to build trust in the government's response, people have to have trust," said Leslie Dach, a Senior Counselor of Health and Human Services during the Ebola outbreak. "Making false promises and them not turning out not to be true undermines people's confidence," Mr. Dach said. He pointed to Mr. Trump's claim in February about the virus that, "We did shut down, yes." As recently as the week of

February 24th, Mr. Trump appeared to simply want to put the coronavirus response in his rear-view mirror. "I think that's a problem that's going to go away," he said in remarks on Tuesday, February 25[th,] to a group of business leaders in New Delhi.

On Wednesday, February 26[th,] before Mr. Trump's news conference, his allies on television and radio appeared to be speaking to the proverbial "audience of one" as they sought to give their unsolicited advice to the president. On Fox News, daytime hosts noted the news conference presented an "opportunity for him to act presidential." Mr. Trump, however, chose to conduct the news conference his own way. "It is what it is," he said of the potential for a virus with a higher fatality than the flu to spread through communities. "We've got the greatest people in the world."

After days of downplaying the global coronavirus threat, President Donald Trump tried to show Americans that his administration is ready to handle a possible outbreak in the USA amid a bipartisan criticism and warnings from his own health officials that the virus is almost sure to spread. Trump, who suggested weeks ago that the threat would go away once temperatures warmed in April, huddled on Wednesday, February 26th, at the White House with officials from the Centers for Disease Control and Prevention to go over the administration's strategy for dealing with the virus. Lawmakers from both parties expressed concern that the administration is not doing enough to prepare for a possible outbreak of the virus that has spawned more than 80,000 cases worldwide, including 59 confirmed cases in the USA.

Health and Human Services Secretary Alex Azar shot down reports that the administration plans to appoint a Czar to lead the coronavirus strategy. Azar assured the House Appropriations Committee that the administration's strategy is working "extremely well." "If it doesn't work or there is a need for a change, then that would be for the president to decide," he said. Trump fired off a series of tweets early on Wednesday, February 26th, in which he said health officials are doing a "great job" in addressing the global health pandemic. On the day before February 25th, he described the epidemic as "very well under control in our country," despite a sharp increase in cases.

President Donald Trump declared on Wednesday, February 26th, that a widespread U.S. outbreak of the new respiratory virus sweeping the globe is not inevitable even as top health authorities at his side warned Americans that more infections are coming. Trump sought to minimize fears as he insisted the U.S. is "very, very, ready" for whatever the COVID-19 outbreak brings. "This will end," Trump said of the outbreak at a White House news conference. "We've had tremendous success, tremendous success beyond what people would've thought," the president said following days of mixed messages, tumbling stocks, and rising death tolls abroad, driven by the coronavirus. Shortly after Trump spoke, the CDC announced a worrisome development. Another person in the U.S. is infected, someone in California who does not appear to have traveled abroad or been exposed to another patient. If the CDC confirms that, it could be a first in this country and a sign that efforts to contain the virus spread have not been enough. "It's possible this could be an instance of community spread of COVID-19," the CDC said in a statement.

More than 81,000 cases of COVID-19, an illness characterized by fever and coughing and, in severe cases, shortness of breath or pneumonia, have occurred since the new virus emerged in China. The latest case from California brings the total number infected in the U.S. to 60, most of them evacuated from outbreak zones. Trump credited border restrictions that have blocked people coming into the U.S. from China for keeping infections low so far. Now, countries worldwide from South Korea and Japan to Italy and Iran are experiencing growing numbers of cases. Asked if it was time to either lift the China restrictions or take steps for travelers from elsewhere, he said: "At the right time we may do that. Right now, it's not the time."

Trump spent close to an hour discussing the virus threat after a week of sharp stock market losses over the health crisis and concern within the administration that a growing outbreak could affect his re-election. He blamed Democrats for the stock market slide, saying, "I think the financial markets are very upset when they look at the Democrat candidates standing on the stage making fools out of themselves." At one point, he shifted to defend his overall record and predict a win in November.

A key question is whether the Trump administration is spending enough money to get the country prepared, especially as the CDC has struggled to expand the number of states that can test people for the virus. Other key concerns are stockpiling masks and other protective equipment for health workers and developing a vaccine or treatment. Health officials have exhausted an initial $105 million in emergency funding and have been looking elsewhere for dollars. Earlier the third week of February, Trump requested $2.5 billion from Congress to fight the virus. Senate Democratic Leader Chuck Schumer of New York countered with a proposal for $8.5 billion.

Chapter 9

President Donald Trump Picks V.P. Pence Crisis Manager to Fight Coronavirus

President Donald Trump's decision to put Mike Pence in charge of the administration's coronavirus response will test the Vice President's ability to manage a rapidly growing crisis as stock prices plunge and critics charge that the administration is not doing enough. As the Trump administration prepares for a potentially broader coronavirus outbreak, one challenge that awaits Pence will be coordinating a response for a president who is prone to second-guessing the advice of experts. During a news conference on Wednesday, February 26[th,] to announce Pence's appointment, Trump contradicted a warning from the Centers for Disease Control and Prevention that the spread of the virus in the United States is inevitable. "I don't think it's inevitable," Trump said. "I think that we're doing a really good job in terms of maintaining borders and turning-in terms of letting people in, in terms of checking people."

Trump's decision to put Pence in charge is a good sign of how the administration prioritizes its response. But having Pence coordinate the effort is "not an appropriate substitute" for someone who could devote their full attention to the issue, such as "Czar" Ronald Klain, who had been appointed during the Obama administration, said Ned Price, spokesman for the National Security Council from the Obama administration. "He still has all of his official duties to carry out unless he's going to take a sabbatical from his role as Vice President. I think it's substituting one problem for another," Price said, noting Pence had spoken at the Conservative Political Action Conference on the same day as his first meeting with the coronavirus task force. Trump signaled confidence in Pence's ability to coordinate the administration's response when he announced the appointment on February 26th. "He's got a certain talent for this," Trump said as Pence stood at his side along with officials from the Centers for Disease Control and Prevention and other agencies. Some questions whether Pence is the right choice argued that health care professionals would be better positioned to monitor and react to a virus that has already spawned more than 80,000 cases worldwide, including 60 in the U.S.

Top officials such as Health and Human Services Secretary Alex Azar and National Institute of Allergy and Infectious Diseases Director Anthony Fauci are "highly qualified" to handle the crisis, said John Holden. He was the Senior Science and Technology Advisor to President Barack Obama. "I just have to wonder whether President Donald Trump will ever be listening," Holdren said.

Asha George, who heads a bipartisan group of former government officials who analyze the U. S's capacity to defend against biological threats, applauded Trump's decision to put Pence in charge of the coronavirus response. Multiple agencies are involved in such an effort, making a coordinated response difficult, said George, Executive Director of the Bipartisan Commission on Biodefense. "You need somebody with enough power and authority to direct everybody and make sure everybody is doing what they're supposed to be doing," she said. "The Vice President carries a lot of weight and is pretty much the only person short of the president who can get this sort of thing done, especially in the midst of a response, as we are now," she said.

Pence announced on Thursday, February 27th, that he had tapped Debbie Birx, who oversees U.S. efforts to fight HIV and

AIDS, to help manage the response to the coronavirus threat. The administration also added three members to its coronavirus task force: Treasury Secretary Steve Mnuchin, Surgeon General Jerome Adams, and National Economic Council Director Larry Kudlow. Pence's selection of Birx could ease the concerns of some lawmakers who called for the Trump administration to put someone with expertise in charge of the federal response. "Debbie Birx is a highly qualified public health expert who is kind of battle-tested," said Tom Frieden, director of the CDC and Commissioner of the New York City Health Department.

Trump's budgets routinely proposed to cut funding for agencies such as the CDC and the NIH that are now on the front lines of the fight against the virus. At a news conference briefing on February 26th, Trump said the coronavirus threat did not make him question those previously proposed cuts. Trump said, "We know all the people. We know all the good people, we can get them back very quickly, if the staff is cut."

Chapter 10

Global Economic Crisis Markets Falling is Fiscal Test for Trump

The global spread at the deadly coronavirus is posing a significant economic test for President Donald Trump. His three year stretch of robust growth could be shaken by supply chain delays, a tourism slowdown, and ruptures in other critical sectors of the American economy. The outbreak of the virus in China has already disrupted global trade, sending American companies and retailers that rely on Chinese imports scrambling to repair a temporary break in their supply chains. Its spread to South Korea, Italy, and beyond has hindered global trade. Economic forecasters say that the effects will hurt growth in the United States in 2020, even if they do not intensify. If the virus becomes a global pandemic, it could knock the world economy into recession.

Stock markets have plunged at the end of February on fears about the virus, with companies such as Apple and Microsoft among the most prominent businesses that have warned that supply chain disruptions could slow sales. Analysts say the February declines were on track to be the steepest since the 2008 financial crisis. The market fall presents a challenge for Mr. Trump, whose presidential success has been deeply tied to the economy and a rising stock market that is now experiencing pronounced jitters. For now, Mr. Trump has publicly played down the potential economic fallout, saying woes at the aerospace giant Boeing, a strike last year at General Motors, and the Federal Reserve's reluctance to slash interest rates have done more to hurt the economy. "We have been hurt by General Motors," Mr. Trump said on February 26th. "We have been hurt by Boeing, and we've been hurt-we've been hurt, in my opinion, very badly, by our own Federal Reserve.

Health officials expect a spike in coronavirus cases in the United States, though it remains unclear how soon and how severe an outbreak might occur. Public health officials in February have warned the nation to be prepared for the virus spread. If the infection gains a significant foothold in the United States, it could keep workers at home and grind production to a halt, hurting revenue streams and taking even highly leveraged corporations as they fall behind in debt payments. In the least severe case, the current slowdown in China could cause a short-lived growth blip. Economists at Goldman Sachs already expects to shave 0.8 percentage points off the United States domestic product in the first three months of 2020 because of slumping tourism from China and trade slowdowns. But they expect a quick rebound that will help make up for the slump in the second quarter. Other economists, including those at Moody's Analytics, foresee a more drastic fallout if widespread infections appear in other countries. A global recession "is likely" if the virus "becomes a pandemic, and the odds of that are uncomfortably high and rising with infections surging in Italy and Korea," Mark Zandi, Moody's Chief Economist, wrote on February 26th.

Perhaps the most important thing the government can do to insulate the economy is to storm the outbreak, keeping Americans on the job and spending. If that fails, fiscal responses are an option. Hong Kong and China, both hit hard, have rolled out packages to help bolster growth. Tax and spending policies might also encourage demand more than fixing supply, but they can also work more quickly than monetary policy. House Speaker Nancy Pelosi of California and Senator Chuck Schumer of New York, the Democratic leader on February 27th called for Congress and Mr. Trump to fashion a spending bill meant to "address the spread of the deadly coronavirus in a smart strategic and serious way." A response should include interest-free loans for "small businesses impacted by the outbreak." Such a program would represent targeted relief but not an effort to increase consumer demand in the economy dramatically. But such a plan seems far-off, if not improbable. Democrats and Republican leaders in Congress have not opened talks with the White House or between the House and Senate over any possible package of tax cuts and spending increases that would be meant to stimulate the economy in the event of a virus-related downturn. Top Senate aides said on February 27th, that it was too soon for such conversations, with Mr. Trump's allies noting the persistence of low unemployment and continued economic growth.

Michael Zona, a spokesman for the Senate Finance Committee and its chairman, Charles E. Grassley of Iowa, said on February 27th that "at this point, the coronavirus has not had a broad impact on the U.S. economy, and its effects have been limited." But Mr. Grassley and the committee were "ready to consider appropriate tax relief if "that becomes necessary and the extent of the problem can be determined." Mr. Trumps' economic advisors had already been working on a package of tax cuts intended to serve as a centerpiece of his 2020 campaign. That package, which is still in flux and probably months away, could include new tax cuts for the middle class and startup businesses, along with extensions of some expiring provisions of the 2017 tax cuts. Tax experts who have spoken with the administration do not see the effort as an immediate stimulus package, but more as an attempt to build on the 2017 law and offer voters a contrast between Mr. Trump and his Democratic opponent.

The coronavirus outbreak began to look more like a worldwide economic crisis on February 28th as anxiety about the infection emptied shops and amusement parks, canceled events, cut trade and travel, and dragged already slumping financial markets even lower. More employers told their workers to stay home, and officials locked down neighborhoods and closed schools. The wide-ranging efforts to halt the spread of the illness threatened jobs, paychecks, and profits. "This is a case where economic terms the cure is almost worse than the disease," said Jacob Kirkegaard, a senior fellow at the Peterson Institute of International Economics. "When you quarantine cities, you will lose economic activity that you're not going to get back."

The list of countries touched by the illness climbed to nearly 60 as Mexico, Belarus, Lithuania, New Zealand, Nigeria, Azerbaijan, Iceland, and the Netherlands reported their first cases. More than 83,000 people worldwide have contracted the illness, with deaths tapping 2,800. Meanwhile, in the U.S., another virus case was discovered in California, and Oregon reported its first case. In California, that means the virus is spreading in at least two separate communities about 90 miles apart, according to health officials. On Wednesday, February 26th, authorities revealed the nation's first case of community transmission, a woman in Solano County, California. There is no apparent connection between the new patient and anyone else with the disease, said Sara Cody, the county's health officer. In Oregon, the infected person worked at an elementary school in the Portland area, which will be temporarily closed, authorities said. "The case was not a person under investigation. The individual had neither a history of travel to a country where the virus was circulating nor is believed to have had close contact with another confirmed case," the two most common sources of exposure," the Oregon Health Authority said in a statement.

China, where the outbreak began in December, has seen a slowdown in new infections and, on February 29th, reported 427 new cases over 24 hours along with 47 deaths. The city at the epicenter of the outbreak, Wuhan, accounted for the bulk of both. New daily cases in mainland China have held steady at under 500 for the past four days, with almost all of them in Wuhan and its surrounding Hubei province. With the number of discharged patients now greatly exceeding those of new arrivals, Wuhan now has more than 5,000 spare beds in 16 temporary treatment centers, Maxiaowei, Director of the National Health Commission, told a news conference in Wuhan on Friday, February 28th.

South Korea, the second hardest-hit country, on Saturday, February 29th, reported 594 new cases, the highest daily jump since confirming its first patient in late January. Emerging clusters in Italy and Iran, which has had 34 deaths and 388 cases, have led to the infection of people in other countries. France and Germany also saw increases, with dozens of infections. The head of the World Health Organization, on Friday, February 28th, announced that the risk of the virus spreading worldwide was "very high," citing the "continued increase" in the number of cases and the number of affected countries. U.N. Secretary-General Antonio Guterres urged all governments to "do everything possible to contain the disease." "We know containment is possible, but the window of opportunity is narrowing," The U.N. Chief told reporters in New York.

President Donald Trump and his aides played down the threat it posed and said Democrats and the media were overhyping the dangers of the outbreak, the Washington Post reported. Senior administration officials tried to project an image of vigilance and preparedness on February 29th. They briefed reporters on the Federal government's latest efforts to contain the virus and expeditiously secure additional funding from congress. Eric Ueland, the White House's Chief Liaison to Capitol Hill, detailed the numerous briefings about the virus that the administration has provided to lawmakers, including conversations with more than 200 congressional offices that began early in January. He said he expected an emergency funding package to clear congress as early as next week, with the goal of Trump signing the additional money into law before lawmakers leave for their mid-March recess. Lawmakers and aides said they intend to work through the weekend to get an agreement on the emergency spending bill.

Negotiations are circling around a $6 billion to $8 billion commitment, with some officials involved saying they anticipate ending up at the higher end of the range, the Post reported. The final figure will dwarf the 2.5 billion spending plan the White House proposed earlier this week. Also, the White House plan included only $1.25 billion in new funding, while taking more than $500 million from an Ebola response fund and other sums from the National Institutes of Health and elsewhere. The congressional spending bill is expected to be all new money. Larry Kudlow, Trump's Top Economic Advisor, said the selloff in markets might be an overreaction to an epidemic with uncertain long-term effects.

Chapter 11

First and Second Death in the U.S., President Trump Reassures Americans "No Reason to Panic."

The governor of Washington declared a state of emergency on February 29th after a man died there of COVID-19, the first such reported death in the United States. More than 50 people in a nursing facility are sick and being treated for the virus. Governor Jay Inslee directed agencies to use "all resources necessary" to prepare for and respond to the coronavirus outbreak. The declaration also allows the use of the National Guard, if necessary. "We will continue to work toward a day where no one dies from the virus," the governor vowed.

Health officials in California, Oregon, and Washington state are worried about the coronavirus spreading through West Coast communities because a growing number of people are being infected despite not having visited an area where there was an outbreak, nor been in contact with anyone who had. The man who died was in his 50's, had underlying health conditions, and no history of travel or contact with a known COVID-19 case, health officials in Washington state said at a news conference. A spokesman for the Evergreen Health Medical Center, Kayse Dahl, said the person died in the facility in the suburb of Kirkland. "In addition, over 50 individuals reported ill with respiratory symptoms or other respiratory conditions of unknown cause and are being tested for COVID-19. A growing number of cases in California, Washington state, and Oregon are confounding authorities because the infected people had not recently traveled overseas or had any known contact with a traveler or an infected person. The U.S. has about 60 confirmed. Worldwide, the number of people sickened by the virus on February 29th was around 83,000, and there were more than 2,800 deaths, most of them in China. A 60-year-old U.S. citizen died in Wuhan, China, in early February.

In Washington, seeking to reassure the American public, President Donald Trump said on Saturday, February 29th, that there was "no reason to panic" as the new coronavirus claimed its first victim inside the United States. The White House also announced new restrictions on international travel to prevent its spread. Trump, speaking only moments after the death in Washington state, was announced, took a more measured approach a day after he complained that the virus was being overblown and that his political enemies were perpetuating a "hoax." "This is very serious stuff," he said, but still insisted the criticism of his administration's handling of the virus outbreak as a "hoax."

Trump appeared at a hastily called news conference in the White House briefing room with Vice President Mike Pence and top public health officials to announce that the U.S. was banning travel to Iran and urging Americans not to travel to regions of Italy and South Korea where the virus has been prevalent. He said 22 people in the U.S. had been stricken by the new coronavirus, of whom one had died while four others were deemed "very ill." Trump said he was considering additional restrictions, including closing the U.S. border with Mexico in response to the virus spread, but later added: "This is not a border that seems to be much of a problem right now." "We're thinking about all borders," he said.

Travel to Iran is already quite limited, though some families can travel there on a visa. It is one of the seven initial counties on Trump's travel ban list, which means travel from Iran is already severely restricted. Robert Redfield, Director of the Centers for Disease Control and Prevention, said there was "no evidence or link to travel" in the case of the man who died. Redford said the CDC mistakenly told Trump in an earlier briefing that the victim was a woman.

On Friday, February 28th, health officials confirmed a third case of coronavirus in the U.S. in a person who had not traveled internationally or had close contact with anyone known to have the virus. The U.S. has had about 60 confirmed cases. Trump's tally appeared to exclude cases of Americans repatriated from China or evacuated from the Diamond Princess cruise ship. Trump said healthy Americans should be able to recover if they contract the new virus, as he tried to reassure Americans and global markets spooked by the virus threat. He encouraged Americans not to alter their daily routines, saying the country is "super prepared" for a broader outbreak, adding "there's no reason to panic at all."

Health officials in Washington State said on the evening of March 1st that a second person had died from the coronavirus, a man in his 70's from a nursing facility near Seattle where dozens of people were sick and had been tested for the virus. Earlier research said the virus might have been circulating for weeks undetected in Washington state, meaning hundreds of undiagnosed cases. Washington state, as of March 2nd, has 12 confirmed cases. Elsewhere, authorities announced the third case in Illinois, and Rhode Island and New York had its' first case. The hospitalized patient in Rhode Island is a man in his 40's who had traveled to Italy in February. New York confirmed March 1st that a woman in her late 30's contracted the virus while traveling in Iran.

As the fallout continued, Vice President Mike Pence and Health and Human Services Secretary Alex Azar sought to reassure the

American public that the federal government is working to ensure state and local authorities can test for the virus. Both said during a round of TV talk show appearances March 1st that thousands of more testing kits had been distributed to state and local officials, with thousands more to come. "They should know we have the best public health system in the world looking out for them," Azar said, adding that additional cases will be reported, and the overall risk to Americans is low. On March 1st, Researchers at the Fred Hutchinson Cancer Research Center and the University of Washington said they had evidence that the virus may have been circulating in the state for up to six weeks undetected, a finding that, if true, could mean hundreds of undiagnosed cases in the area. At the time, they posted their research online, but it was not published in a scientific journal or reviewed by other scientists.

Scientists not affiliated with the research pointed out that for many people, especially younger, healthier ones, their symptoms are not much worse than the flu or bad cold. "The symptoms are pretty nonspecific, and testing criteria has been pretty strict, so those combinations of factors mean that it easily could have been circulating for a bit without us knowing," said Justin Lessler, an Associate Professor of Epidemiology at John Hopkins Bloomberg School of Public Health. Dr. Adam Louring of the University of Michigan called the findings "high-quality work."

Pence, named by the president to oversee the government response, said more than 15,000 virus testing kits had been released over the last weekend of April through March 1st. The administration is working with a commercial provider to distribute 50,000 more, Pence said. Azar said, more than 3,600 people have been tested for coronavirus, and the capability exists to test 75,000 people. Washington state emerged as the U.S. center of a spreading coronavirus fight, as state health officials reported four additional deaths there, 18 confirmed cases, and multiple schools closed for disinfection. March 2nd deaths involved three women in their 70's or 80's linked to an outbreak at the Life Care Center nursing facility in Kirkland, Washington, and one man in his 40's from neighboring Snohomish County. The nursing home was the site of four of the nation's deaths and had other confirmed cases, including one woman in her 80's who was in critical condition.

New cases were also reported in California, Oregon, Massachusetts, New Hampshire, and Illinois on March 2nd as state officials attempted to quell fears. At least 50 people have been diagnosed with the novel infection within the U.S. as of March 2nd, not including repatriated Americans. The onset of local testing and expansion of testing criteria helped lead to identifying new cases of COVID-19 disease in the U.S., stoking concerns over a wider spread of the virus, and prompting governors and state health officials to take extra measures to prevent further transmission.

On Saturday, February 29th, local health officials in Seattle said that delays in testing for the virus had slowed identification of community cases, meaning those who did not travel to places with significant outbreaks or have contact with known patients. "If we had the ability to test earlier, I'm sure we would have been able to identify patients earlier," said Dr. Jeffery Duchin, Health Officer for Seattle and King County. In the first case in Washington, the man in his 30's had been traveling in Wuhan, China, and returned home to Snohomish County, Washington, on January 15th. He sought medical care a few days later after developing symptoms and suspected that he might have the coronavirus, officials have said, and the test later comes back positive. Health officials had scrambled to retrace his history, tracking down eight people he had socialized with at a group lunch and 37 who were in the clinic when he showed up for medical help. They also reached out to people on his flight back to the United States. But as the man remained in hospital isolation, and then later returned home, officials reported no new cases in Washington state. They tested two dozen people over five weeks, and all came back negative. That changed the last week of April when the state laboratory became able to test for the virus. Officials reported two new confirmed cases on the evening of February 28th, and then more, including the first patient to die of the virus in the United States. They then began working to trace how the cases in the state might be linked, and who else might have been exposed.

Health officials in Washington state, where a particularly troubling cluster of cases surfaced at a nursing home outside Seattle, said four more people had died from the coronavirus, bringing the number of deaths to six, all in Washington. Over 100 cases have been confirmed in the U.S. as of March 2nd, with more in the coming weeks. Thousands of test kits were on their way to state and local labs, and new guidelines intended to expand screening were put in place.

Chapter 12

Testing Capabilities Struggle, Demand for Test Kits Falls Short

The Trump administration has struggled to project confidence and progress in the fight against the coronavirus and simultaneously prepare Americans for what could be a difficult struggle. The slow start in testing for the virus has been an uphill struggle for the administration. Officials at the White House emphasized that the supply of tests may not fully meet demand until the coming weeks in March. They said that around 2,500 test kits or more than one million individual tests could be available by the weekend of March 6th. An additional million tests could be manufactured weekly after that. "We are trying to meet the demand with increased capacity," Dr. Stephen Hahn, the Commissioner of the Food and Drug Administration, told reporters during the briefing. "Right now, I'd say we'd need more capacity." On March 7th, the FDA gave laboratories and hospitals the go-ahead to conduct tests previously limited by the CDC (which had been enforcing strict guidelines about who was allowed to be tested). Vice President Mike Pence said the Centers for Disease Control and Prevention lifted all restrictions on testing for the coronavirus and would be releasing new guidelines to fast-track testing for people who fear they have the virus, even if they are displaying mild symptoms.

Dr. Hahn said at a Senate hearing that the CDC was working with a private manufacturer to increase the testing capacity of laboratories across the nation drastically. "Our expectation in talking to the company that is scaling up is that we should have the capacity by the end of the week (March 6th) to have kits available to the laboratories to perform about a million tests," he said. Dr. Hahn was then asked to clarify; he said he was hearing from private manufacturers that 2,500 test kits could be available by the end of the week, with each kit capable of 500 tests. Later in the day, Mr. Pence repeated that number to reporters, saying the kits amounted to 1.5 million tests. Dr. Hahn said, "this is a dynamic process; every day we're hearing from additional manufacturers." But under questioning from Senators in both parties, Mr. Pence, who is heading the administration's coronavirus response, and other top health officials were unable to satisfy lawmaker's concerns. "They could not answer how soon people would be able to get tests," said Senator Chuck Schumer of New York, the Democratic leader. "We need an on-site test, not a test that has to be sent far away and sent back, and we need to know where people can get it, how people can get it."

The package, which has been quickly put together over the past few days, is expected to be larger than the White House's initial proposal: $1.25 billion in new funds, paired with a transfer of existing funds from other health programs. Since the evening of March 2nd, new infections in Westchester County, New York; San Mateo County, California; Wake County, North Carolina; and Fulton County, Georgia, made clear that the coronavirus was spreading in America's largest urban centers and was no longer tethered to international travelers. In the United States, there have been at least 120 cases of coronavirus confirmed by lab tests as of the evening of March 3rd, and worldwide infections neared 93,000.

The number of tests administered in the coming days could be substantially lower than the administration's projection of one million by the week of March 9th. A spokesman for the Department of Health and Human Services said that on March 9th public labs currently can test 15,000 people and could test up to 75,000 by the end of this week (March 8th). The Association of Public Health Laboratories, which represents state and local government laboratories around the country, has said that its labs would be able to conduct about 10,000 tests a day when all its 100 members can perform testing. Scott Becker, the Executive Director of the Lab Association, said on March 2nd that labs could run about 100 tests per day. As of March 2nd, he said fewer than half of those labs were able to do so. "All that matters is how many people you can test a day," said Scott Gottlieb, the FDA Commissioner from 2017 to 2019.

As they learned on March 3rd, that the death toll in their state had reached nine, the two Democratic senators from Washington pressed Mr. Pence and the health officials about both the administration's response and its message to the public, particularly about the availability of testing. "Our message to them was, be clear that they aren't readily available, and the universe of people who have access to them is not large enough," Senator Maria Cantwell said. "Let's figure out a more aggressive plan." The state's other Senator, Patty Murray, said she had been hearing from constituents who were desperately calling "every number they can find" for information, and cannot get through. "I think there's a lot of concern about the honest, accurate reflection of what is real when you have something like this happening, "Ms. Murray said. She criticized the Trump administration's efforts to play down the effects of the virus.

"What I really feel strongly about is, we do not need Mick Mulvaney telling people don't watch TV," she added, referring to remarks made by the acting White House Chief of Staff. "We do not need the president saying this fear-mongering." Dr. Anthony Fauci, The Director of the National Institute of Allergy and Infectious Diseases, told in an interview on February 28th that Americans should expect the outbreak to worsen. "I don't think that we are going to get out of this completely unscathed, I think that this is going to be one of those things we look back on and say, "boy that was bad." Dr. Fauci also said that he would be truthful in his public pronouncements, even as President Trump sought to minimize the virus impact. "You should never destroy your own credibility. And you do not want to go to war with a president," Dr. Fauci said. But you got to walk the delicate balance of making sure you continue to tell the truth.

States on the front lines of the coronavirus fight are complaining about the availability of test kits, exposing strains in the nation's battle to contain the epidemic. New York City's Deputy Mayor for Health, Raul Perea-Henze, struck an urgent tone in a letter on March 6th to the Centers for Disease Control and Prevention, saying the test kits provided to the city do not meet its needs. "Slow federal action on this matter has impeded our ability to beat back this epidemic," he wrote. As of Friday, March 6th, 94 people had been tested in New York City, according to the city's health website. Nearly 2,800 are in quarantine, officials said, and the city needs to be able to test hundreds a day. The CDC was contacted but did not respond to a request for comments.

The CDC is now shipping hundreds of test kits as of March 6th. Some public health labs and private lab companies have also rolled out their own test kits. Large commercial lab companies, including LabCorp and Quest Diagnostics Inc., are launching coronavirus testing services. This has increased the capacity to test samples to thousands of people a day. A marked improvement from the relative few the CDC was able to evaluate at its Atlanta laboratories. At the same time, it tried to work out the kinks in a test it had developed. Yet the improvement isn't enough, public health experts and government officials say, especially after the CDC recently broadened the criteria for testing to anyone who shows signs of symptoms, had traveled to a country with an outbreak, or came in contact with a confirmed case.

Public health officials in King County, Washington, have called testing capacity inadequate in the state, where all but one of the U.S. coronavirus deaths have taken place. "We've been waiting for an increase in testing capacity in our community. It has been a tremendous strain for public health to triage those tests," said King County Executive Don Constantine at a March 6th briefing. Officials in Washington state were hopeful for more testing capacity soon, though not necessarily from the federal government. But even as New York City said it did not have enough, New York state officials said the state has enough test kits for the moment. The state can test about 500 samples a day, said Governor Andrew Cuomo, at a briefing on March 6th, and it hopes to increase its capacity to 1,000 samples a day. The bottleneck was laboratory capacity, not test kits, Mr. Cuomo said.

About 4,000 people in New York state are in quarantine and being monitored for symptoms of the virus, state officials said on March 6th. The number of people in the state with the infection rose to 44 on March 6th, officials said. The number was 22 on March 5th. The goal in the U.S. was to get to a point where people with symptoms can be tested quickly, but that has proven to be a big challenge. "We are not at the point now," said Tom Inglesby, Director of the Center for Health Security of the John Hopkins Bloomberg School of Public Health, said at a March 6th briefing on Capitol Hill, "We don't have the bandwidth to do that now." U.S. Food and Drug Commissioner Stephen Hahn said at the same press conference that as of Thursday, March 5th, the CDC had shipped out supplies for about 900,000 tests. Another 200,000 are expected to be shipped on Saturday, March 7th. Testing requires more than one specimen per patient, so the number of people who could be tested with the supplies is fewer. "We don't have enough tests today to meet what we anticipate will be the demand going forward," acknowledged Vice President Mike Pence, who is leading the administration's response to the outbreak.

The Health and Human Services Department did not immediately respond to the request for comment on March 6th. Health and Human Services Secretary Alex Azar said on March 6th that the federal government had provided Washington and California states, which have some of the highest numbers of cases, with all the tests they requested. The CDC has shipped tests capable of testing as many as 75,000 people to public health labs, and as many as four million tests could be ready by the week of March 9th. "The production and shipping of tests that we've talked about all week are completely on schedule," Mr. Azar said at the White House.

Before the first week of March, few public health laboratories were able to conduct tests. The CDC halted shipments of a test it had developed because the test was malfunctioning, and the FDA had not given laboratories authority to develop, validated, and use their own tests. Tests have come online since then because the CDC dropped a malfunctioning component, and the FDA streamlined its authorization process. Public health labs have received hundreds of CDC test kits in the first few days of March, and thousands more are expected, said Scott Becker, Chief Executive of the Association of Public Health Laboratories, who represents about 150 state and local public health labs. Each kit can perform tests on specimens for hundreds of patients. About 69 public health labs in the U.S. had on-site test capacity as of March 6th, with more expected over the weekend, up from eight a week ago, Mr. Becker said. He expects the labs will soon have the capacity for testing about 10,000 people a day across the U.S.

President Trump claimed again on Friday, March 6th, that anyone who needed a coronavirus test "gets a test." But from Washington state to Florida to New York, doctors and patients are clamoring for tests that they say are in woefully short supply, and their frustration is mounting alongside the growing number of cases around the country. In California, only 516 tests had been conducted as of March 5th. Washington health officials have more cases than they can currently process. In New York, where cases have quadrupled the week of March 5th, a New York official pleaded for more test's kits from the CDC. "The slow federal action on this matter has impeded our ability to beat back this epidemic," the official said in a letter on March 5th.

Now, more than 300 cases have been confirmed, at least 14 have died, and thousands are in self-quarantine. Public health officials warn that no one knows how deeply the virus will spread, in part because the federal government's flawed rollout of tests three weeks ago in April has snowballed into an embarrassing fiasco of national proportions.

Chapter 13

Virus Grows, Mitigation Needed, Pandemic Causing a New Reality

As the coronavirus spreads to two-thirds of the states, Americans begin to grasp the magnitude of the threat facing them. The weekend's case tally ballooned, veering toward nearly 600 cases and close to 20 deaths in the U.S. In Washington state, with the epicenter in the Seattle area, Governor Jay Inslee said on March 8th that he was considering mandatory measures to help keep people apart. Federal public health officials also signaled that the degree of community spread, with new cases popping up with no known links to foreign trade, indicated that the virus was beyond so-called containment in some areas and that now, stricter measures should be considered.

It is a concept in public health known as shifting from containment of an outbreak to "mitigation," which means acknowledging the tried-and-true public health message of isolating the sick and quarantining their contacts are no longer enough. Steps must be taken to minimize deaths from the disease and slow its spread so that hospitals are not overwhelmed: Dr. Anthony Fauci, Director of the National Institute of Allergy and Infectious Diseases, told Fox News on Sunday, March 8th, "And that's the reason we've got to be prepared to take whatever action is appropriate to contain and mitigate the outbreak," Trying to control the outbreak spread of this virus by having all people be in a lockdown is not what the American people want to hear, but the fact of isolation, to keep people affected by the virus away from getting contaminated, is a real hard fact, and must be taken seriously, especially in big cities where the infection has taken hold.

If community spread is being detected now the first week of March, that means it began without being seen, weeks if not months ago. The main concern is for older people, particularly those with underlying health conditions like diabetes, heart disease, lung problems, and weakened immunity. For vulnerable people, Dr. Fauci said: "Don't wait for community spread. Now is the time to social distance, whether there is spread in your community or not." The goal of mitigation is at least to slow down an epidemic. "If you can stretch things out long enough, you buy more time for the development of the vaccine and the research to be done for treatments."

Along with New York and Washington, California has the highest number of people infected with the virus. Less than 1,000 people have been tested for the coronavirus in California, and about 120 had tested positive. As the state ramps up its testing capabilities in the coming days, it is expected and confirmed that the virus would increase. As of March 4th, the U.S. death toll from the new coronavirus grew to 11, with California announcing its first fatality linked to the viral infection and Washington state reporting its 10th death. Recent cases are also being reported across both coasts. Local and federal governments moved to calm fears, provide resources, and make recommendations to vulnerable populations and employees to help combat the spread. The number of confirmed coronavirus cases globally exceeded 105,000 on March 9th, as infections spread to new parts of the U.S., and Italy quarantined some 17 million people to get a handle on the epidemic. At least eight states have declared states of emergencies, granting governors additional powers to combat the spread: New York,

California, Florida, Kentucky, Maryland, Utah, Washington, and Oregon, which declared it on Sunday, March 8th.

In Washington, top officials warned that the epidemic was now in the broader circulation, and the older people with underlying conditions are at risk and should stay home. On Sunday, March 8th, health officials raised the death toll in Washington to 18, with 16 of those linked to Life Care Center of Kirkland, including 15 residents and other residents were in the process of getting test results, six of whom were ill.

Some former government officials pointed out that the Trump administration was not acting quickly enough to corral the virus from spreading. Dr. Scott Gottlieb said on TV on March 8th that the federal government needed to step up quickly. "There's no systematic plan of when a city should close schools or when they should tell businesses that they have to telework, we leave these decisions to local officials, but we should have a comprehensive plan in terms of recommendations to cities and some support from the federal government for cities that make that step, make that leap if you will."

The W.H.O. declared the coronavirus to be a global pandemic on March 11th as stock markets accelerated their plunge, schools, universities, businesses, theaters, and sports stadiums shut their doors. Millions of people cut themselves off from their regular lives. With infections and fear rising, President Trump planned to address the nation at 9 pm on Wednesday, March 11th. New York shifted state colleges to online classes, Washington state banned gatherings like parades and concerts, and Seattle shuttered its schools.

Mr. Trump and other world leaders struggled to find a way forward. A day after he called for calm and assured Americans that the virus "will go away," Mr. Trump declared on March 11th that he was "fully prepared to use the full power of the Federal Government" to confront the virus. But by early evening on March 11th, he was still at loggerheads with congressional leaders on how to respond. Governors chose not to wait for Washington. Governor Andrew M. Cuomo of New York said that the state-run university system and the city university and colleges, with about 100,000 students, would shift primarily to online classes starting March 19th.

The toll of the health crisis on the economic prospects of the United States and other countries was clear that the virus is starting to be a reality that is difficult to deal with by the U.S. and other countries. The Dow Jones industrial average was down 20% from its peak, officially ending the 11-year bull market that began after the financial crash of 2008. Mr. Trump huddled with advisors and banking executives and said, "I am fully prepared to use the full power of the Federal Government to deal with our current challenge of the coronavirus!" Speaking with reporters during a White House meeting with bankers, the president expressed surprise that Democrats were skeptical of a payroll tax cut, not mentioning that many Republicans likewise were wary. "If we get rid of the problem quickly, everything solves itself," he said. "We are thinking about various forms of stimulus."

Mr. Trump dismissed critics who have said he has not appeared to take the crisis seriously enough or matched his statements to those of health experts. "That's CNN, fake news," he said angrily. With the White House and Democrats divided over what a broader economic stimulus package should look like. The two parties appeared to be coalescing around the idea of a narrower short-term bill focusing on paid leave, enhanced unemployment insurance, food assistance, and help for small businesses. There would still be much more discussion over other economic measures, like tax cuts and rescue plans for affected industries. But this would wait until Congress returns from a weeklong recess.

Steven Mnuchin said he would recommend to Mr. Trump that the Internal Revenue Service delay payments without penalty or interest for all Americans other than the super-wealthy. Mr.

Mnuchin noted that all individuals could request tax filing extensions online, but that this would be a special provision meant to help small and midsized businesses and "hardworking individuals" dealing with the fallout from the coronavirus. Dr. Fauci and other health officials were given the responsibility to sound the alarm that Mr. Trump seemed unwilling to voice himself. "We must be much more serious as a country about what we might expect," Dr. Fauci told the House Oversight and Reform Committee. "We cannot look at it and say, "Well, there are only a couple of cases here, that is good. Because a couple of cases today are going to be many, many cases tomorrow."

Dr. Robert R. Redfield, the Director of the Centers for Disease Control and Prevention, said, "This is the time for everyone to get engaged." Representative Mark Green, Republican of Tennessee, said, "The 24/7 criticism the president is undergoing is unwarranted at a minimum." Representative Gerald E. Connolly, Democrat of Virginia, showed a picture of the president wearing a campaign hat while visiting the CDC, "We will not be lectured about politicization, and all of our wards and sanctimony will not cover up the fact that this administration was not prepared for this crisis and put lives, American lives, at risk," he said.

Chapter 14

Trump Declares National Emergency but Says, "I Don't Take Responsibility at All."

President Donald Trump declared a national emergency to confront the spread of the coronavirus on Friday, March 13th, as his administration reached an agreement with House Democrats on a bipartisan economic relief package for Americans affected by the global pandemic. The announcement was made in the Rose Garden. He repeatedly praised his handling of the crisis, and he denied responsibility for his administration's missteps and said for the first time, he would likely undergo testing for the coronavirus. "In addition to opening up access to $50 billion and a large amount of money for states and territories and localities," he said, adding that he had reached a new partnership with private companies to "vastly increase and accelerate our capacity to test for the coronavirus."

The virus outbreak has proved to be one of the most challenging episodes of Trump's presidency. "We are doing a great job, and we have 40 people right now, 40, compare that with other countries that have many, many times that amount," Trump said. The administration has been taking increasingly aggressive steps to contain the outbreak after criticism that not enough is being done to address the public health threat facing the country, with as of Friday, March 13th, the number of deaths had risen to 48. Trump predicted that while up to 5 million additional tests are in the pipeline, the United States will not need nearly that many. "We want to make sure that those who need a test can get a test very safely, quickly, and conveniently, but we don't want people to take a test if we feel that they shouldn't be doing it and we don't want everyone running out and taking one if they only have certain symptoms," Trump said. The emergency declaration was the most far-reaching federal action to date to respond to the fast-spreading outbreak of disease that has not yet reached its peak in the United States. The coronavirus has sickened more than 144,000 worldwide and had killed nearly 5,400 by Friday, March 13th. The number of infections is likely much higher.

After facing heated bipartisan criticism, the Trump administration announced a series of steps to boost the availability of tests and said it would partner with the private sector to set up drive-through testing sites. The move was a tactic acknowledgment by Trump that his week-old assertion that tests were available to anyone who wanted them had yet to become a reality. That claim has been belied by criticism from lawmakers and frustrated Americans unable to determine whether they are infected. Trump was reluctant to take ownership of the problems that have led to a lack of available tests and confusion about who is eligible to use the limited supply at hand. "I don't take responsibility at all," Trump said, blaming his predecessors, and saying he knew nothing about his administration's 2018 decision to disband a team of experts who had focused on preparing for global pandemics. As Congress and the administration struggled to develop a stimulus package that all sides would agree to that would combat the virus. European officials announced a series of aggressive measures to support their economies and try to contain the viruses spread.

The World Health Organization declared Europe the center of the pandemic. European Union officials announced they would allow member nations to run larger than average budget deficits to stimulate economic growth during the outbreak. France and Germany announced stimulus plans. In the United States, Mr. Trump moves at the possibility of Congress sending a comprehensive bill to the president's desk bringing progress in the effort to slow the spread of the virus and minimize its growing damage to the economy.

But they still fell short of the steps that a growing number of economists say lawmakers must take to confront a crisis with little precedent in American history. When the stock trading closed on Friday, March 13th, the president followed his emergency declaration by introducing new uncertainty about the scope and speed of the government's fiscal responsibility. "We don't think the Democrats are giving enough in negotiations," he said, regarding an emerging compromise to provide paid leave, safety net benefits, and other measures meant to help consumers and businesses weather the sharp slowdown in economic activity that is threatening to grip the country. After Mr. Trump's remarks, a senior administration official said that he was referring to his interest in securing nearly $1 trillion temporary cuts in payroll taxes, an idea that lawmakers from both parties have viewed with skepticism.

The House was planning to vote on March 13th on the proposal, including a sweeping new paid sick leave provision, enhanced unemployment benefits, free virus testing, and additional funds for food assistance and Medicaid. The Senate is expected to take it up and pass it in a week. "As the Senate works to pass this bill," Pelosi wrote to colleagues, "the House will begin work on a third emergency response package to protect the health, economic security, and well-being of the American people.

Mr. Trump sent mixed messages about the size of the economic impact he was expecting, and the steps Americans should take to avoid contracting or transmitting the virus. He called on Americans to make "short-term sacrifices" like avoiding large gatherings and postponing business travel, and he warned that the next eight weeks would be critical for slowing the spread of the virus. "This will pass, though, and we're going to be stronger for it," Mr. Trump said.

A new, high-speed coronavirus test was earlier granted emergency clearance by the Food and Drug Administration. Developed by Roche Holding AG, the test is designed to run on the company's automated machines, which are already installed in more than 100 laboratories across the U.S., it will be available immediately. By the week of March 16th, Mr. Trump said, there would be a half-million additional tests available, with five million tests available within a month. The emergency declaration will also allow key federal agencies to waive rules that could hamper the response to the outbreak, Mr. Trump said, including limits on how hospitals can treat and accommodate patients with the virus.

Similar moves are also being made in Europe. World Health Organization Director-General Tedros Adhanom Ghebreyesus on Friday, March 13th, called the epicenter of the new coronavirus outbreak. The number of cases tapped 136,800 in 123 counties and regions around the globe. "More cases are now being reported every day than were reported in China at the height of the epidemic," he said. Spain said it would declare a state of emergency after the number of cases in the country increased quickly to more than 4,000, making it the second biggest epicenter of the pandemic in Europe after Italy. Italy, which is under an unprecedented nationwide quarantine, reported over 2,500 new cases on March 13th for a total of 17,660. The death toll rose by 250 to 1,266.

On Tuesday, March 24[th,] President Donald Trump said he hopes to scale back the nation's dramatic response to the coronavirus pandemic within weeks to revive the economy and pack churches by Easter Sunday. This inspiration was panned by public health experts and many elected leaders, including Republicans. "I would love to have the country opened up and raring to go," Trump said during a Fox News town hall broadcast from the White House Rose Garden. The Easter holiday is on April 12th.

The president's push to restart the faltering U.S. economy goes against the advice of experts who continued to warn that the correct restrictions might need to stay in place for months to take away any further increase of American deaths. His views also clashed with medical workers alarmed at the prospect of hospital emergency rooms being utilized to the maximum with not enough room to accommodate the critical virus patients, governors who have ordered more than 100 million Americans to stay home, some members of his own party, and world leaders who have pursued much more aggressive measures to slow the pandemic. Trump appeared at a briefing in the late afternoon of March 24th, where he initially struck a much different tone about the decisions that lay ahead. Reading from a prepared statement, Trump vowed to listen to public health experts before changing his course about the country's relaxing restrictions. "Our decision will be based on hard facts and data, rest assured, every decision we make is grounded in the health, safety, and well-being of our American citizens.

But the president can read from prepared statements to appease the viewers and make himself look like a president making wise statements. Still, the president returned to the rosiest of scenarios, saying the country was "beginning to see the light at the end of the tunnel." He talked of how congress seemed on the brink of passing a $2 trillion stimulus, even though the bill was still in process. Treasury Secretary Steven Mnuchin and congressional leaders were engaged in final negotiations.

Trump's optimism about how quickly American life could return to normal also collided with a darkening reality. On March 24th, the number of confirmed cases of COVID-19 in the nation surpassed 50,000, continuing a rapid rise. More than 600 American deaths have been blamed on the disease. The epicenter of the outbreak has shifted to the New York metropolitan area, which accounts for half of the U.S. cases and where the disease is spreading faster than anywhere in the country. Globally, the tally of confirmed cases eclipsed 400,000, as the infection continues to increase. New York topped 25,000, and the number of infections is doubling every three days.

"You can destroy a country this way, by closing it down," Trump said in a broadcast from the Rose Garden, comparing the current outbreak to other factors that kill Americans each year. "We lose thousands and thousands of people a year to the flu, but we don't turn the country off. We lose much more than that to automobile accidents. We do not call the automobile companies and say, stop making automobiles. These analogies have been with us for years, and we have learned to live with them as reality and address them."

The World Health Organization once established the mortality rate at 3.4%. However, Fauci, a vital member of the president's coronavirus task force, had more recently indicated it was closer to 1%, still about ten times worse than that of the seasonal flu. Some political allies pushed back on Trump. "There will be no normally functioning economy if our hospitals are overwhelmed. Thousands of Americans of all ages, including our doctors and nurses, lay dying because we have failed to do what is necessary to stop the virus," Representative Liz Cheney, R-Wyoming, wrote on Twitter. Scott Gottlieb, the Trump administration Food and Drug Administration Commissioner from 2017 to 2019, said it would be impossible to be a stable economy amid a deepening epidemic, so long as COVID-19 spreads uncontrolled. Older people will die in historic numbers, middle-aged folks are doomed to prolonged ICU stays to fight for their lives, hospitals will be overwhelmed, and most Americans will be terrified to leave homes, eat out, take the subway, or go to the park," he wrote in a Twitter message late Monday, March 23rd.

In Ohio, Governor Mike DeWine, a Republican, became the latest leader from Trump's party to affirm that saving lives must take priority over returning the U.S. economy to full force. "Protecting people and protecting the economy are not mutually exclusive," DeWine said during his daily briefing on the virus outbreak. "The fact is, we save our economy by first saving lives. And we have to do it in that order."

Chapter 15

Three Phase Plan Unveiled
but Not Followed by Trump

President Donald Trump gave the governor's a road map on April 16th for recovering from the economic pain of the coronavirus pandemic. The plan laid out "a phased and deliberate approach" to restoring normal activity in places that have robust testing and are seeing a reduction in the coronavirus (COVID-19). "We're starting our life again; we're starting rejuvenation of our economy again, this is a gradual process."

The three-phase plan aims to ease restrictions in areas with low transmission of the coronavirus while holding the line in harder-hit locations. It was made clear that returning to everyday activities will be a far longer process than Trump initially seen. Federal officials warn that some social distancing measures may need to remain in place through the end of the year to prevent another outbreak. The plans already initiated by governors will be reinforced with the public health organizations in their states. Trump told the governors on April 16th that "You're going to call your own shots, we're going to be standing alongside of you," this was according to a recording obtained by the press.

In Phase 1, the plan recommends strict social distancing for all people in public. Gatherings larger than ten people are to be avoided, and nonessential travel is discouraged. In Phase 2, people are encouraged to maximize social distancing and limit gather-ings to no more than 50 people unless precautioning measures are taken, travel could resume. Phase 3 envisions a return to normal everyday life for most Americans, focusing on the identification and isolation of any new infections. Trump said recent trends in some states were so positive that they could almost immediately begin taking the steps laid out in Phase 1. "They will be able to go literally tomorrow," Trump said.

Governors of both parties made clear they will move at their own pace. Some governors said that guidelines seem to make sense. West Virginia Governor Jim Justice, a Trump ally, cau-tiously floated the idea of reopening parts of the state but said testing capacity and contact tracing would have to be considerably ramped up before restrictions could be softly lifted. "All would be forgotten very quickly if we moved into a stage quicker than we should, and then we go into a situation where we had people dying like flies," Justice said.

In briefing governors on the plan, Trump said they would be responsible for deciding when it is safe to lift restrictions in their states. Just days before, Trump had drawn swift pushback for claiming he had absolute authority to determine how and when states reopen. "We have a large number of states that want to get going, and they're in very good shape, that's good with us frankly," Trump said. Trump, on April 16[th,] claimed the U.S. has "built the most advanced and robust testing anywhere in the world." But people close to him warned more would be necessary. South Carolina Senator Lindsey Graham said on ABC television, "We are struggling with testing at a large scale, you really can't go back to work until we have more test." Former Vice President Joe Biden, Trump's likely opponent in November's presidential election, said on April 16th that Trump "kind of punted." This was all being said by Trump with the COVID-19 cases and deaths continuing to go higher every day. As of April 16th, the number of daily cases in the U.S. was at 26,034, and the number of daily deaths was at 1,278.

"We're not going to be able to really make significant changes in the three phases the presidents talking about until we're able to test much more broadly," Biden said. There was also concern that the White House was taking too rosy a view on the trends in the U.S. "I would not declare a peak almost anywhere in the U.S. yet," said Mark Lipstich, a Harvard Epidemiology Professor. He recommended "working to enhance surveillance and testing, so if we hit a peak, it will be possible to identify with greater certainty." But some of Trump's conservative allies have encouraged him to act swiftly, warning him of "a mini Great Depression if we keep the economy shut down.

On April 17th, President Donald Trump amplified his call to reopen the country. Trump suggested that citizens "liberate" themselves even as governors and local officials were not ready to return to normal. They showed significant concern about opening up too soon, especially with the COVID-19 expanding its spread in the United States. Republican governors have been slow to embrace Trump's call to lift statewide stay-at-home orders amid the pandemic that is killing thousands of Americans. The question must be asked, why does President Donald Trump want to lift the stay at home requirements? There appears to be no reason to proceed with such an action, as the current rate of cases and deaths are increasing. There is a lack of federal leadership in a response effort plagued by shortfalls in testing and equipment.

On April 17th, Texas announced a plan for loosening restrictions on economic activity. "We'll be focusing on all strategies that may open up Texas. While also keeping us protected from the expansion of COVID-19," Governor Greg Abbott said, announcing plans to ease restrictions on some retail and hospitals even as the state's stay-at-home order remained in effect. Trump, on April 17[th,] aimed at Democratic-led states and tweeted about the need to "liberate" places such as Michigan, Minnesota, and Virginia, while appearing to agree with protestors in these locations which are rebelling against restrictions that are the same Trump administrators social distancing recommendations. With the rebellions taking place, several governors in recent days have taken steps to reopen their states' economies gradually, while including caveats that maintain social distancing rules.

In addition to Texas, Vermont will undergo a "phased restart" of its economy beginning April 20th, Republican Governor Phil Scott said. Minnesota's Democratic Governor Tim Walz said outdoor activities, including boating and hiking, can resume as businesses, including golf courses, shooting ranges, and bait shops open their doors. Montana Governor Steve Bullock, a Democrat, said a lifting of restrictions would begin April 24th, in phases, because "once we begin to reopen, we want to be able to stay open." Trump has focused most of his criticism on Democratic governors, including another tense back-and-forth on April 17th with New York's Andrew Cuomo. Republican officials may be the president's most significant obstacle in his push for a quick reopening in parts of the country where the coronavirus outbreak has been more limited. Governors eager to rescue their economies and feeling heat from President Donald Trump are moving to ease restrictions meant to control the spread of the coronavirus, even as new hotspots emerge, and experts warn that moving too fast could prove disastrous. Adding to the pressure is the stay-at-home order protest organized by small-government groups and Trump supporters. They staged demonstrations April 18th in several cities one day after the president urged them to "liberate" three states led by Democratic governors.

For the first time in weeks, people could visit some Florida beaches, but they were still subject to restrictions on hours and activities. Meanwhile, the infections kept surging after the mandate to "liberate" was proclaimed by Trump. Trump, whose administration waited months to bolster stockpiles of critical medical supplies and equipment, appeared to back protesters as stated earlier. "LIBERATE MINNESOTA!" "LIBERATE MICHIGAN" "LIBERATE VIRGINIA," Trump said in a tweetstorm in which he lashed out at New York Governor Andrew Cuomo, a Democrat, for criticizing the federal response. Cuomo "should spend more time 'doing' and less time 'complaining,'" the president said.

In Texas, several hundred people rallied on the steps of the Capitol to call for an end to social restrictions. Many of the protesters sought an immediate lifting of restrictions and chanted, "Let us work!" In a state where more than 1 million people have filed for unemployment since the crisis began. Trump has wanted states to relax restrictions by May 1st and has inaccurately claimed "total" authority to decree how that happens. Many governors have long made clear they will ease restrictions at their own pace.

Republic governors urged on by President Donald Trump, are taking the first steps toward reopening parts of their state's economies amid the coronavirus pandemic, and without adhering to the president's guidelines. Democratic governors are largely keeping strict stay-at-home orders and nonessential business closures in place, resisting small pockets of Trump-aligned protesters and public pressure from the president.

Chapter 16

Trump Rarely Listens
When Science Speaks

President Donald Trump spoke words of praise for the scientific minds of the doctors and scientific researchers in March at the Centers for Disease Control and Prevention. "Every one of these doctors, 'How do you know so much about this?' Maybe I have a natural ability," Mr. Trump said. Mr. Trump repeatedly boasted, even with the current pandemic, contradicting medical experts in favor of his own judgment with disregard for scientific advice, which defines his administration.

The world is facing one of its worst health disasters in many generations and needs a leader who is willing to listen and utilize the input the scientific minds provide. The White House administration has diminished the conclusions of scientists in formatting policy. Mr. Trump often puts his political instincts ahead of facts. "Donald Trump is the most anti-science and anti-environment president we've ever had," said Douglas Brinkley, a presidential historian at Rice University. The president's actions, he said, have eroded one of the United States' most desirable assets, the government's deep scientific expertise, built over decades. "It's extraordinarily crazy and reckless," he said.

Once in office, Mr. Trump's administration quickly began work on one of its most far-reaching policies, the systematic downplaying or ignoring of science. The administration faces enormous challenges in controlling the outbreak. Health experts have converged on a broad agreement that sending people back to work too soon, before measures of an extensive testing system is in place, brings risks of new spreading of infection, adding to the existing number of cases and deaths. The Trump administration's guidelines are trying to be followed based on scientific understanding. Experts with scientific knowledge have warned that Mr. Trump's frequent calls to reopen the economy quickly threatens the vital scientific health message given to Mr. Trump in late April. With much of the nation staying home, commerce coming to a halt, and unemployment levels not seen in quite some time, causing turmoil in the financial markets, the motivation to restart the economy has become the main drive of President Donald Trump, rather than the coronavirus, which is growing in cases and deaths in the U.S. and the world.

The pandemic has not slowed the administration's safeguard for health and the environment. The parallels between the administration's environmental rollbacks and its coronavirus response are not exact. When it comes to the coronavirus outbreak, there is still an essential counterweight to many of Mr. Trump's impulses. Most notably, Dr. Fauci, who was asked in April if he thought experts at the National Institute of Health, we're unable to speak their minds or oppose Mr. Trump, Dr. Fauci was unequivocal. "Absolutely not," he said.

With the coronavirus growing in cases and taking deaths daily, there have been some significant staff shake-ups at health agencies. Before the pandemic began, the CDC had reduced its staff in Beijing from about 47 to 14 under the Trump administration. A move that critics have said may have complicated its ability to confront the outbreak earlier. An agency spokesman said it had been done to focus more on "technical collaboration" with China, which requires fewer people.

In February, as mentioned earlier, Nancy Messonnier, a top CDC official, was removed from overseeing the agency's coronavirus response. Dr. Messonnier had warned that Americans needed to prepare for a "significant disruption" at a time when Mr. Trump was insisting that the virus was "very well under control in our country." Rick Bright, on the third week of April, was dismissed as the Director of the Biomedical Advanced Research and Development Authority, the agency involved in work on coronavirus treatments. Mr. Bright said he had been removed after urging caution in expanding access to hydroxychloroquine, the controversial treatment embraced by Mr. Trump. He said the administration had put "politics and "cronyism" ahead of science, he "never heard" of Dr. Bright. Mr. Deere, the White House spokesman, accused critics of waging a campaign "to criticize" this president for discussing anything that might provide hope to the American people. Yet even with Dr. Bright's comments, Trump acknowledged several times that he's "not a doctor," but has previously suggested various ideas for fighting the coronavirus. Trump repeatedly prompted the drug hydroxychloroquine to say such drugs could be a potential "game-changer" in the fight against the virus. On April 24th, the Food and Drug Administration warned that people should not take chloroquine and hydroxychloroquine to treat COVID-19 outside of a hospital or formal clinical trial, citing reports of "serious heart rhythm problems."

On Thursday, April 24th, President Donald Trump suggested at a White House briefing that an "injection inside" the human body with a disinfectant like bleach or isopropyl alcohol could help combat the virus. "And then I see the disinfectant, where it knocks it out in a minute," Mr. Trump said after a presentation from William N. Bryan, acting under Secretary for Science at Homeland Security, detailed the virus's possible susceptibility to bleach and alcohol. "One minute," the president said. "And is there a way we can do something like that, by injection inside or almost a cleaning?

Because you see it gets in the lungs, and it does a tremendous number on the lungs. So, it would be interesting to check that." After Trump's statement, many callers flooded a health hotline with questions that the states Emergency Management Agency had to issue a warning that "under no circumstances" should any disinfectant be taken to treat the coronavirus. In Washington state, officials urged people not to consume laundry detergent capsules. Across the country, health professionals sounded the alarm.

Chapter 17

Pompeo and Trump Ties Virus to China Lab with no Conclusions

Secretary of State Mike Pompeo, on May 3rd, backed President Trump's assertions that the coronavirus originated in a research laboratory in Wuhan, China. However, the nation's intelligence agencies say they have not concluded on the issue. Pompeo said that "there's enormous evidence" that the coronavirus came from the lab. However, he agreed with the intelligence assessment that there was no indication that the virus was man-made or genetically produced. The theories are not mutually exclusive. Some officials who have examined the intelligence reports, which remain classified, say a COVID-infected laboratory animal was destroyed. A lab worker was accidentally infected in the process, which is only one of many theories still being examined.

Mr. Pompeo repeatedly accused China's Communist Party, led by President Xi Jinping, of covering up evidence and denying American experts access to the research lab, the Wuhan Institute of Virology. Mr. Pompeo is among the small group of senior officials believed to be pushing American spy agencies to find evidence to support the theory that the government laboratory in Wuhan was the origin of the outbreak. The Chinese government has vigorously denied that the virus leaked from the laboratory, and at one point, suggested that the American military created it.

The office of the Director of National Intelligence stated on April 30th that it was continuing to "rigorously examine emerging information and intelligence" to determine whether the outbreak began with infected animals or whether it was the result of an accident at a laboratory in Wuhan. On April 30th, Mr. Trump said he had a high degree of confidence that the laboratory was the source of the outbreak, but when pressed for evidence, Trump said, "I'm not allowed to tell you that." Mr. Trump is the final authority on declassifying evidence, and he had done so when it suited his purposes. There is concern by some of the intelligence analysts that the pressure from administration officials could distort the final assessments about the virus's origin. Intelligence could be used as a political weapon in an intensifying battle with China over a disease that has infected more than three million people worldwide. If the administration continues the path that Mr. Pompeo and Mr. Trump have made hot news in recent days, they will doubtless come under increasing pressure to make available some of the evidence that led them to their conclusions. Some evidence appears to be based on electronic intercepts of communication among Chinese officials. Mr. Trump and Mr. Pompeo are probably going to say they cannot risk revealing sources and methods of intelligence collection.

"I can tell you that there is a significant amount of evidence that this came from that laboratory in Wuhan," Mr. Pompeo said May 3rd, on ABC. During a Fox News appearance on May 3rd, President Trump suggested China engaged in a cover-up because they were embarrassed. "I think they made a horrible mistake, and they didn't admit it," Trump said. "We're going to be giving a very strong report as to exactly what we think happened," Mr. Trump said of questions about the Wuhan lab. "I think it will be very conclusive." Mr. Trump said he has seen intelligence reports from China and the virus but declined to elaborate. China's role in spreading the virus continues to be debatable without conclusive evidence presented to the American people.

Chapter 18

As States Reopen, More Deaths are Coming, Short of Minimum Testing

S tates across the country are moving swiftly to reopen their economies despite failing to achieve benchmarks laid out by the White House for when social distancing restrictions could be eased to ensure the public's safety during the coronavirus pandemic. White House recommendations released in April encouraged states to wait to see a decline in cases over a two-week period and have robust testing in place for frontline workers before entering "Phase One" of a gradual comeback. But states such as Texas, Indiana, Colorado, and Florida have pushed forward with relaxing social distancing guidelines.

President Donald Trump and some of his aides have backed away from their own guidelines, opting instead to hail the broad economic reopening that health experts say has started too quickly. The White House appears to distance itself from its own government report predicting coronavirus cases will surge to about 200,000 per day by June 1st, a jump that would be accompanied by more than 3,000 deaths per day. The White House and the Centers for Disease Control (CDC) and Prevention disputed the report, although the slides carried the CDC logo. The report said 100,000 cases per day by the end of May is within the realm of possibility, an indication that cases could spiral out of control at the same time the White

House has shifted focus toward reopening the economy. "There are reopening scenarios where it could get out of control very quickly," said Justin Lessler, an Associate Professor of Epidemiology at the John Hopkins Bloomberg School of Public Health, who created the model. The Bloomberg school in a statement called the report a "preliminary" analysis that should not be used as a forecast. The White House doom played the figures saying they have not been closely analyzed. "This data is not reflective of any of the modeling done by the task force, or data that the task force has analyzed, "White House Judd Deere said in a statement.

About a third of the states continue to see their number of new coronavirus cases increasing, compared to a few that have seen a sustained decline. The national trend shows where the rate of new cases has leveled off in recent weeks but has not declined. Most governors who have decided to open up are not following the letter of the White House guidelines. As of the first week of May, 1.2 million people have been confirmed as infected by the coronavirus, and more than 68,000 have died in the United States. Both figures are widely believed to undercut the actual totals. The White House continues to support its guidelines in hopes of reducing the cases and deaths. The White House wants local officials to take the lead in deciding how quickly to ease restrictions, according to a senior administration official who spoke on the condition of anonymity to discuss internal deliberations.

Congressional leaders are girding for a massive fight over the re-entry of millions of Americans to the workplace. President Donald Trump has increasingly focused on pushing businesses to reopen. The White House received a CDC reopening document by the nation's top disease investigators, which gave a step by step process to local authorities on how and when to reopen restaurants and other public places during the outbreak of the coronavirus. The 17-page report by the Centers for Disease Control and Prevention team titled "Guidance for Implementing Opening up

America Again Framework" was researched and written to help church leaders, business owners, educators, and state and local officials as they begin to reopen. The report was supposed to be published May 1st, but the agency scientists were told the guidance report "would never see the light of day," according to a CDC official. The Trump administration has been closely controlling the release of guidance and information on the new coronavirus with the president himself leading freewheeling daily briefings in which the White House buried the CDC report.

Traditionally, it's been the CDC's role in giving the public and local officials guidance and science-based information during any public health issue. Still, during this pandemic, the CDC has not had a leading role in nearly two months, with the CDC Director Dr. Robert Redford being mostly absent from public appearances. "CDC has always been the public health agency Americans turn to in time of crisis," said Dr. Howard Koh, a Harvard professor and former health official. The White House was asked about the CDC report. Apparently, the guidelines have not been stopped and were still in the editing phase to be more simplified to satisfy President Donald Trump.

As the states begin their relaxing of being on lockdown from the coronavirus, there are minimum levels of testing prescribed by the federal government that the states are falling short. Three months into the coronavirus health emergency, the White House has not answered calls about the need for a coordinated plan to conduct millions of tests that are needed to contain the virus. The analysis found that most states are not meeting the testing required based on the number of people that must be tested. If states do not have a testing system that can accommodate all to be tested, the ability to detect further outbreaks when they occur will lead to more spread without detection to be able to contain the spread of the coronavirus.

Testing in many states has been limited to hospitalized patients, high-risk individuals, and frontline workers. Containing the virus will require a massive expansion of testing that would include millions of patients without symptoms, which currently is not happening because the Trump administration lacked any metrics state officials could use to make decisions based on the results. The documentary provided by the federal government was straightforward that the states are responsible for testing; the federal government is supposedly the "supplier of the last resort." The closest the White House has come to issuing a benchmark does not appear in the document. Senior administration officials said the government would provide each state with enough test swabs and related materials to screen at least 2.6% of their population in May and June of 2020. States hit harder by the outbreak would be eligible for additional assistance. The 2.6% figure was unclear on how it was determined; officials with the U.S. Department of Health and Human Services explained it as 2% of state populations per month without explaining the discrepancy. There was no answer when asked whether the administration has a target for how many daily tests should be done nationwide or when they would issue more details.

Only about 40% of states currently meet even the 2% testing threshold. The percentage is expected to rise as states increase their testing capabilities. A White House spokesman said May 1st that the administration's testing threshold is only a suggestion, and states are ultimately responsible for deciding how to reopen in a "safe and responsible manner." The administration said it is working on expanding testing and highlighting plans that were first announced in March for additional testing sites at retail pharmacy chains. Some states which have moved aggressively to ease opening restrictions and lifting stay-at-home orders are just under the 2% threshold. Louisiana and Kansas, where Republican lawmakers are pressuring governors to reopen, are falling short of the requirements for testing. In Kansas, the governor and top health administrators expect to reach the 2% mark the first week of May, and Florida, which just started its first phase of reopening, also fell short but said they would be able to test 30,000-40,000 people a day if needed.

Prior health officials and experts were critical of the federal government's blueprint. They said the 2.6% or 2% of the population number was too vague and did not consider guidelines from the Centers for Disease Control (CDC) on who should be tested. By not defining who should be tested, it is unknown if they should test everybody or just ones with symptoms and all their contacts. Doctors were confused, and they are saying, "If that amounts to 2%, that's fine, but the guidelines are not to test 2%. The guidelines are to test who needs it." Many experts already say the national testing rate falls short of what is needed to ease social distancing guidelines safely. Researchers at Harvard have calculated that the U.S. needs to be testing roughly 500,000 people per day before considering easing restrictions starting in May. That is a nearly 150% increase from the recent daily tally of approximately 200,000 tests.

The United States is under criticism for not having done enough to test the population for coronavirus infections as cases increased significantly. President Donald Trump claimed on May 11th that his administration is the best in the world in testing and that it will help states expand their testing, which are the key elements having to lift the safety restrictions that have closed much of the economy since March. Trump claimed, "We have met the moment, and we have prevailed." He said the United States should pass 10 million completed tests the week of May 11th, "nearly double the number of any other country." Officials outlined the plan in front of giant banners that proclaimed, "America leads the world in testing." Trump said that with the federal help, each state would be able to test more people per capita in May than South Korea has tested in four months.

The White House event on Monday, May 11th in the afternoon amounted to an acknowledgment that there is not yet enough testing capacity across the United States even as more than 40 states are in some stage of lifting restrictions on travel, work, and school. The president claims about U.S. testing benchmarks do not account for what health experts have criticized as the slow pace of testing capability in the United States this spring, a delay that some attribute to the rapid spread of the virus, the mounting death toll, and uncertainty about the way forward. "Testing is absolutely critical and is the only way to get back in any safer form," said Eileen O'Connor, a spokeswoman for the Rockefeller Foundation, which has been working with companies and governmental leaders on increasing testing. "Unless you have the data, you don't know where the disease is going."

Administration officials said that states were asked to detail their needs and capacities and that the $11 billion in aid would be distributed to meet those testing needs. A map displayed in the Rose Garden suggested that two hard-hit states, New York and New Jersey, would get the highest level of spending. Other states with significant levels of infection, includes Michigan, Florida, Illinois, and California, are expected to reach between $300 million and $500 million each. The United States, as of Sunday, May 10th, had completed nearly 9 million coronavirus tests, while an enormous number, equivalent to 2.74% of the U.S. population it does not give a full representation of the viruses reach within American Society.

There are far higher levels of per capita testing in other parts of the world. In tiny Iceland, the figure is 15.4%, but that amount is about 54,000 tests across a population of 352,000 people. Likewise, in other industrialized economies with large outbreaks also have fared better in testing than the United States. Italy has conducted tests equivalent to 4.3% of its population, and Germany is at 3.35%. The United States is also still behind its northern neighbor, Canada, where its 1.09 million tests are now equivalent to 2.95% of its population. Data from the COVID Tracking Project details how the country has slowly increased its daily testing over time. Since the beginning of May, the United States has reported more than 250,000 tests on most days. On May 11th, the country reached a record of nearly 395,00 tests. Those figures remain far below the volume that many health experts say will be essential before schools and businesses can reopen before Americans can safely gather, go to work, and travel again.

On the week of May 4th, public health researchers at Harvard University's Global Health Institute published new estimates arguing that the United States needs to be conducting at least 900,000 tests daily by May 15th to have a better grasp of the out-break. Other researchers have predicted that the nation would need to perform as many as several million tests a day to handle the viruses spread. The Harvard findings said fewer than a dozen states are testing enough to keep ahead of the virus. Most other researchers wrote that they are not testing at a level that will allow them to adequately track people who get sick and others they come into contact with. While Trump moves to increase testing, the United States continues to be, by far, the world's coronavirus hotspot. There have been 1.34 million confirmed cases through May 9th, more than the sum of cases in Spain, the United Kingdom, Italy, France, and Germany. U.S. deaths passed 80,000 on Monday, May 11th.

Chapter 19

Nation's Top Infectious Disease Expert Urges Slow Reopening

Anthony Fauci, the nation's top infectious disease expert, warned of "suffering and death that could be avoided" and further economic damage if states reopen too quickly. He said the U.S. death toll from the coronavirus is likely higher than the 80,000 reported in the middle of May. His comments came during highly anticipated Senate testimony on Tuesday, May 12th, as he and other leading federal health officials were pressed on whether the country is ready to reopen. The panel chairman and witnesses were appearing remotely in an unusual session that includes the first congressional testimony from Fauci, a vital member of the White House task force, selected by President Donald Trump when he declared the coronavirus crisis a national emergency on March 13th.

Appearing with Fauci are Stephen Hahn, head of the Food and Drug Administration, Robert Redfield, Director of the Centers for Disease Control and Prevention, Brett Giroir, and Assistant Secretary at the Department of Health and Human Services. These individuals appeared before the Republican-led Senate Health Education, Labor, and Pensions Committee, which is titled "COVID-19: Safely Getting Back to Work and Back to School." But Democrats are also seizing the opportunity to focus on short-comings in the Trump administration's response. GOP Senator

Lamar Alexander of Tennessee, the panel's chairman, began the questioning by asking Fauci whether college and school administrators could feel safe, welcoming students back to campus in the fall, and the likelihood of a treatment or vaccine becoming available by then. "The idea of having treatments available or a vaccine to facilitate re-entry of students into the fall term would be something that would be a bit of a bridge to fat," Fauci said. "The drug that has shown some degree of efficiency was modest and was in hospitalized patients," Fauci said. Whether students will feel safe returning to school will largely depend on testing capabilities.

Giroir said he expects the country to have the capacity to conduct 25 million to 30 million tests a month by the fall, which could allow schools to have a surveillance strategy in place to identify and isolate confirmed COVID-19 cases quickly. This statement was made even though researchers at Harvard have calculated that the U.S. needs to be testing roughly 500,000 people per day before easing restrictions starting in May. If schools are included as part of the 25 to 30 million tests available in May, then the 500,000 people per day is feasible. The recent daily total is 200,000 tests, so increasing to 500,000 would be nearly a 150% increase.

Democratic Senator Patty Murray of Washington pressed Fauci. Fauci warned that states that fail to obey federal reopening guidelines and move too quickly to restart their economies would put themselves at risk of new outbreaks that could be hard to control. "If some areas, cities, states, or what-have-you jump over these various checkpoints and prematurely open up without having the capability of being able to respond effectively and efficiently, my concern is that we will start to see little spikes that might turn into outbreaks," said Fauci. "I have been very clear in my message to try to the best extent possible to go by the guidelines, which have been very well thought out and very well delineated." Any loosening of restrictions, Fauci added, would lead to new cases, but those new cases could be manageable so long as states have the proper infrastructure in place. "It's the ability and the capability of responding to those cases with good identification, isolation, and contact tracing, that will determine whether you can determine whether you can continue to go forward as you try to reopen America," he said.

Murray also pressed Giroir, the federal official overseeing the coronavirus testing efforts, on a strategic testing plan required to be submitted later in May to Congress under the terms of recent legislation. Giroir said that the administration had numerical targets in place for testing each state but cautioned that hey stand to be revised based on the course of the viruses spread. "Yes, there will be targets, the targets will need to change based on the evidence that we see. So, we really just need to be very humble about this. We need to look at the data," he said. Fauci said the U.S. death toll is probably higher than the 80,000 deaths officially reported and added that the virus would not disappear in the fall or winter, contradicting President Trump's claims the first week of May, that the virus would go away even without a vaccine. "I feel about vaccines like I feel about tests: This is going to go without a vaccine," Trump said on May 8th, adding that there could be "flareups," including in the fall, but that COVID-19 would go away regardless. "That is just not going to happen," Fauci said of the idea that the virus would disappear on its own. "It's a highly transmissible virus. It is likely there will be a virus somewhere on this planet that will likely get back to us." Fauci also agreed with Vermont Senator Bernie Sanders, who said many experts have said that the death toll is higher than what has been reported.

Chapter 20

Trump had Three Years to Prepare Pandemic Strategies

For the first three years of his presidency, Donald Trump did not publicly say the words "pandemic" or "preparedness." Not in speeches, rallies, or his many news conferences planned or last minute. But on May 15, 2020, the White House pointed to extensive planning exercises the administration conducted and reported the threat in 2018. Trump has repeatedly said that the blame for the federal government having inadequate stockpiles of crucial supplies and equipment needed to cope with an outbreak was put on his predecessor, Barack Obama. Obama has been a consistent thwart for Trump on several issues. Still, in the case of planning for the pandemic, he has devoted little attention to the 69-page "playbook" from the Obama administration about the threat of a viral outbreak that might include Ebola or an airborne respiratory illness like coronavirus. The Obama administration could draw from a similar document written during the administration of George W. Bush in 2006.

The politics of pandemic planning have gotten increasingly pitched as the COVID-19 death toll in the country as of August 11, 2020, tops 163,000 American lives. Trump claims he inherited a "broken, terrible" system from Obama. President Donald Trump had three years in office to prepare with more time, enough time to build on the pandemic strategies he inherited. Trump, in an event held outside the Oval Office, declared: "I inherited nothing. I inherited practically nothing from the previous administration, unfortunately."

Beth Cameron, who worked on pandemic planning in the Obama administration, said the playbook that the Obama administration presented to the Trump administration "was given, briefed, and discussed with the incoming administration, explicitly." Cameron said it was intended to provide the White House with a set of questions it should ask early on in an emerging epidemic or pandemic threat. "It outlined who should come together to answer those questions and to be prepared to anticipate what was coming next to get moving," Cameron said. She said the Trump administration was slow to respond to COVID-19, and Obama's playbook could have helped the administration get ahead of an emerging threat like the coronavirus. She said the Bush and Obama administration both did extensive planning for pandemics, and many of those plans were passed to the Trump White House, "They were not political. They were nonpartisan," she added.

The White House Press Secretary Kayleigh McEnany referred to Obama's plan as a "thin packet of paper" replaced by "two detailed, robust pandemic response reports" commissioned by the Trump administration. Her comments drew criticism from Ron Klain, who was the U.S. Ebola response coordinator during the Obama administration. "Let's get to the bottom line," Klain tweeted after McEnonys briefing. "If their position now is that they HAD a plan and that THIS was their plan, I fail to see how that is a helpful argument for them in any way."

The Trump administration's 36-page National Biodefense Strategy, issued in September 2018, was a self-described "call to action." Among the many goals was bolstering preparedness to save lives through "medical countermeasures," such as vaccines, ventilators, diagnostic testing, and personal protective equipment like medical gowns and masks that were in short supply in the early days of the pandemic. McEnany said the nation's stockpile was insufficient but did not answer questions about why Trump did not work to restock it during the first three years in office. The White House said the stockpile had only 28% of the items needed during a pandemic and contained less than a one-month supply of critical items. Still, the administration is updating inventories and how they are distributed.

"President Trump has been in office for well over three years now, which is more than enough to build upon the pandemic strategies he inherited," said Lawrence Gostin, a public health expert at Georgetown University who worked with the Bush and Obama administration on global health issues. "It's quite evident that whatever pandemic planning had been done during Bush or Obama administrations never made it to high levels in the Trump administration." Gostin thinks Trump was just focused on other issues and that pandemic planning wasn't a top priority for the president. Gostin said he was startled when Trump first said that no one expected a pandemic like COVID-19 to happen. "Well, Mr. President, every global health expert, expected this to happen."

Chapter 21

How to Beat the Virus
Until Vaccines Arrive

In just weeks, we could almost stop the viral fire that has swept across this country over the past six months and continues to rage out of control. It will require sacrifice but save many thousands of lives. We believe the choice is clear. We can continue to allow the coronavirus to spread rapidly throughout the country, or we can commit to a more restrictive lockdown, state by state, for up to six weeks to crush the spread of the virus to less than one new case per 100,000 people per day. That's the point at which we will limit the increase in new cases through aggressive public health measures, just as other countries have done. But we're a long way from there right now. The imperative for this is clear because, as a nation, what we have done so far hasn't worked. Some 166,000 people have died (as of August 10, 2020), and in recent days, roughly a thousand have died a day.

On January 30, 2020, when the World Health Organization declared COVID-19 a public health emergency, there were 9,439 reported cases worldwide, most in China, and only six reported cases in the United States. On July 30, six months later, there were 17 million cases reported worldwide, including 676,000 deaths. The United States had four million reported cases and 155,000 deaths. More than a third of all U.S. cases occurred during July alone. The next six months could make what we have experienced so far seem like just a warm-up to a greater catastrophe. With many schools and colleges starting, stores and businesses reopening, and the beginning of the indoor heating season, new case numbers will grow quickly.

Why did the United States COVID-19 containment fail, particularly compared with the successful results of so many nations in Asia, Europe, and even our neighbor Canada? Simply, we gave up our lockdown efforts to control virus transmission well before the virus was under control. Many other countries didn't let up until the number of cases was significantly reduced, even in places with extensive outbreaks in March and April. Once the number of new cases in those areas was driven to less than one per 100,000 people per day as a result of their lockdowns, limiting the increase of new cases was possible with a combination of testing, contract tracing, case isolation, and extensive monitoring of the positive tests.

The United States recorded its lowest seven-day average since March 31st, on May 28th, when it was 21,000 cases or 6.4 new cases per 100,000 people per day. This rate was 7 to 10 times higher than the rates in countries that successfully contained their new infections. While other countries are now experiencing modest flare-ups of the virus, their caseloads are in the hundreds or low thousands of infections per day, not tens of thousands, and small enough that public health officials can largely control the spread. In contrast, the United States reopened too quickly and is now experiencing around 50,000 or more new cases per day.

While cases are falling in the hard-hit areas of Arizona, California, Florida, and Texas because of some physical distancing measures, they are rapidly increasing in a few midwestern states. In Minnesota, we just documented the newest cases in a one-week period since the pandemic began. At this level of national cases, -17 new cases per 100,000 people per day-we simply don't have the public health tools to bring the pandemic under control. Our testing capacity is overwhelmed in many areas, resulting in delays that make contract tracing and other measures to control the virus virtually impossible.

Don't confuse short-term case reductions in some states as permanent. We made that mistake before. Some have claimed that the widespread use of masks is enough to control the pandemic, but let us face reality: Governor Gavin Newsom of California issued a public masking mandate on June 18th, a day when 3,700 cases were reported in the state. On July 25th, the seven-day daily case average was 10,231. We support the wearing of masks by all Americans, but masking mandates and soft limitations on indoor crowds in places such as bars and restaurants are not enough to control this pandemic. To successfully drive down our case rate to less than one per 100,000 per day, we should mandate sheltering in place for everyone but the truly essential workers. By that, we mean people must stay home and leave only for crucial reasons: food shopping and visits to doctors and pharmacies while wearing masks and washing hands frequently.

According to the Economic Policy Institute, 39% of workers in the United States are in essential categories. The problem with the March-to-May lockdown was that it was not uniformly stringent across the country. For example, Minnesota deemed 78% of its workers essential. To be effective, the breakdown has to be as comprehensive and strict as possible. If we are unwilling to take this action, millions of more cases with many more deaths are likely before a vaccine might be available. In addition, the economic recovery will be much slower, with far more business failures and high unemployment for the next year or two. The path of the virus will determine the course of the economy. There won't be a robust economic recovery until we get control of the virus. If we do this aggressively, the testing and tracing capacity we've built will support reopening the economy as other countries have done, allowing children to go back to school and citizens to vote in person in November. All of this will lead to a stronger, faster, economic recovery, moving people from unemployment to work. There is no trade-off between health and the economy. Both require aggressively getting control of the virus. History will judge us harshly if we miss this life-and-economy-saving opportunity to get it right this time.

Chapter 22

Theory on When COVID-19 Will End

There have been many theories on the COVID-19 coronavirus regarding the concept of how it might end. Throughout history, theories have sometimes proved to be correct by using statistics to demonstrate an approach. The results ended up showing stated facts with numbers which were collated daily, which indicated a pattern that logically ended in a way that would conclusively show that a valid group of results remained constant for a prescribed period. COVID-19 is currently statistically followed by several sources that vary in some degree on the numbers but are all reasonably in the same range of changing numbers that reflect the output. The COVID-19 statistical number being documented by the many sources show the daily number of cases and deaths in the United States and the world.

Following the COVID-19 statistics from June 17, 2020, through August 17, 2020, there has been a distinct category that stands out to show a pattern, the daily United States coronavirus deaths (see Figure 1.1 thru Figure 1.7). When looking at this bar chart (see Figure 1.1), there is a distinct pattern that goes up and down, almost like a roller coaster, or for the more technical person, a 60 cycle AC sign wave (see Figure 1.2). When the United States Daily Deaths go down to a low three-digit number, within two to five days after the low number of Daily Deaths, they climb to a four-digit number, as shown in Figure 1.1. This four-digit number might continue to go up until after a few days and then returns to a low three-digit number. During the period from June 17th to August 17th, this pattern is dominant. It will continue if the Federal Government and the States don't take actions to follow strict laws on wearing masks, social distancing, crowd gatherings, and more, per the plan laid out by the Coronavirus Task Team, which is headed up by Vice President Pence.

The cycle that I am describing will continue and, in many instances, will grow and not stop until our leaders, both federal and local, take a stance and accept the ongoing virus as serious. They must make a significant move to enact corrective actions to protect the American people. COVID-19 can be statistically documented into eight categories that clearly define where the United States and the world stand statistically to the cases and deaths which show total numbers for the U.S. and world. The eight categories are:

1) Total U.S. cases
2) Daily U.S cases
3) Total U.S. deaths
4) Daily U.S deaths
5) Total world cases
6) Daily world cases
7) Total world deaths
8) Daily world deaths

These categories change daily and vary cyclically depending on the variance of changes that COVID-19 and its impact changing in the U.S. and world population.

Determining if the coronavirus is weakening will depend on the changing of the eight categories and how they statistically change daily. The ideal number that will show that the virus is slowing is if all eight categories go down from the previous in all eight categories. But if the numbers go up in a specific way or all categories, the cycle will occur and, as mentioned earlier, will continue in a cycle.

All eight categories change daily and vary in a cycle up and down depending on the COVID-19 variance under each category. The ideal statistical number that would be great to see is if all categories go down in numbers and none go up (8 down, 0 up), which is the ideal statistical number that would be the best indicator that COVID-19 is weakening. If the numbers keep going up in some of the major categories, a cycle will occur, showing that all eight categories are moving in a positive or negative direction. The cycle from June 17, 2020-August 17, 2020, was predictable. During this period, eight down and zero up was never seen, along with seven down and one up, and six down and two up, which also never occurred during this period. When the statistics of eight, seven, and six show as going up and are then seen going down, the conclusion can be reached that the virus is slowing. From June 17, 2020, through August 17, 2020, the results are as follows:

Category	**Occurrences**
8 down 0 up	0
7 down 1 up	0
6 down 2 up	0
5 down 3 up	1
4 down 4 up	15
3 down 5 up	6
2 down 6 up	17
1 down 7 up	7
0 down 8 up	14

What are we looking for? We are looking for all eight categories to go down to where none is going up in that group. This is achievable but will require extreme discipline, which other countries that were under extreme government control were able to do, reducing deaths and, in some cases, almost eliminate the pandemic so life could continue, with minimum restrictions.

When reading the COVID-19 book, and getting to this last chapter, the reader would have seen what China and other countries went through, and how COVID-19 was a pandemic that needed attention by the leaders of these countries. As other countries followed the process of rules and regulations, they saw a reduction and, in some cases, an elimination of the virus due to following dictated rules. The current numbers for COVID-19 in the United States as of August 17, 2020, is 5,404, 115 total cases with 42,505 daily cases, and 170,052 total U.S. deaths. The total deaths on June 17, 2020, was 661. When will all this end? The hope is that a vaccine will be developed with therapeutics; what the statistics will be looking for is to achieve a goal of all eight categories going eight down and zero up for a period of one week. If this happens, then statistically, COVID-19 will be close to being defeated.

Figure 1.1 – 1.3 – United States COVID-19 Deaths (DAILY)

Figure 1.1

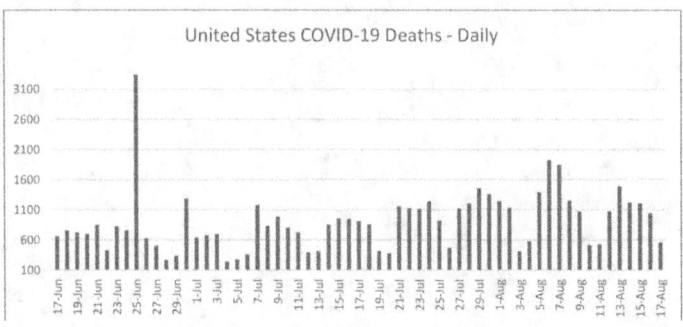

Figure 1.2

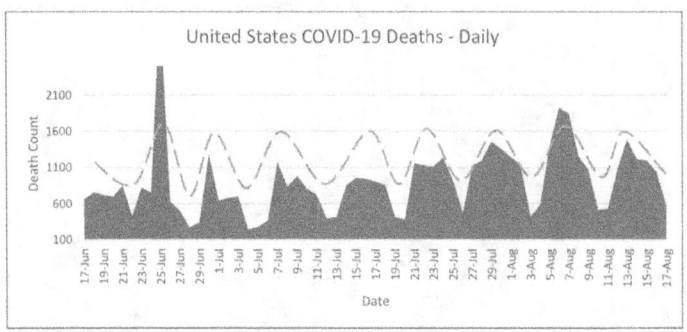

Figure 1.3

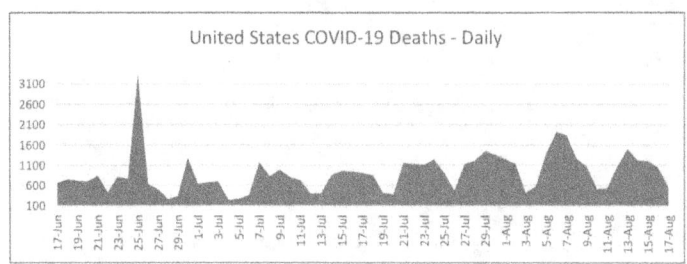

Figure 1.4

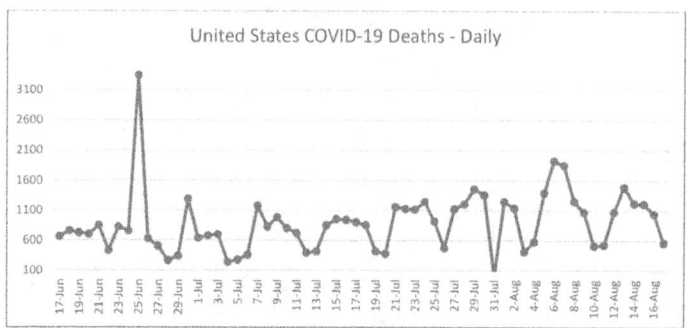

Figure 1.5 – U.S. Cases/Deaths – (TOTAL)

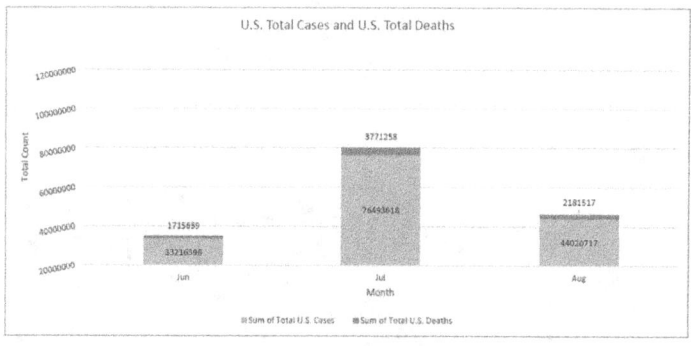

Figure 1.6 – World COVID-19 Cases – (DAILY)

Figure 1.6

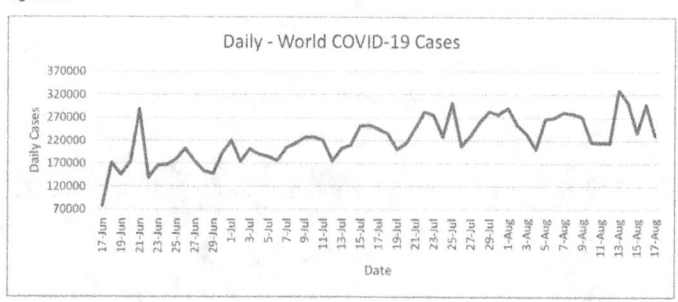

Figure 1.7 – World COVID-19 Deaths – (TOTAL)

Figure 1.7

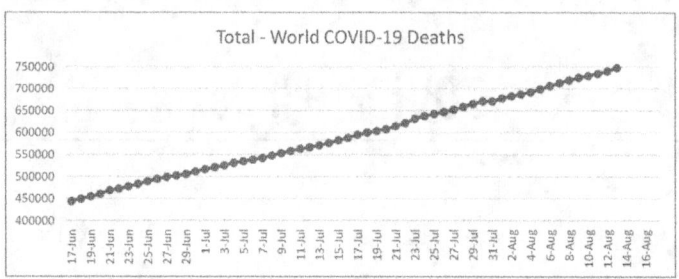

Figure 1.8 – World COVID-19 Deaths – (TOTAL)

Figure 1.8

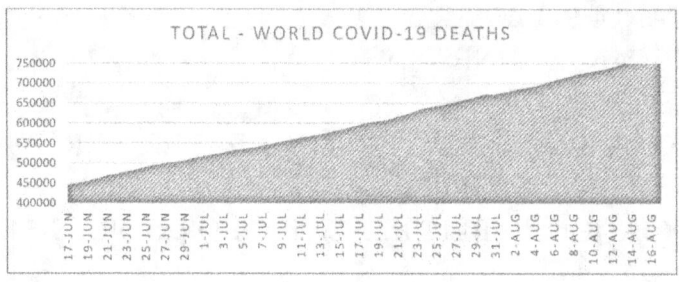

Figure 1.9 – World COVID-19 Deaths – (TOTAL)

Figure 1.9

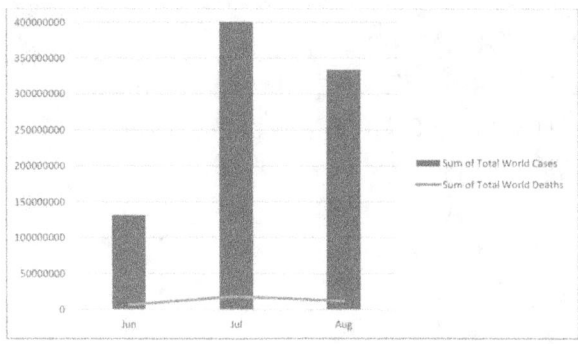

COVID-19 Index

A's
ABBOTT, GREG- 69
ABBVIE, INC.-15
ABC-68, 75
ADAMS, JEROME-42
ALEXANDER, LAMAR-35,81
AMERICAN AIRLINES-8, 95
APPLE-95
ARIZONA STATE UNIVERSITY CENTER FOR PUBLIC HEALTH LAW & POLICY-5
ASSOCIATION, PUBLIC HEALTH LABORATORIES-54, 57
AUSTRIA-34
AZAR, ALEX-VIII, 5, 8, 38, 41, 50, 56

B's
BEACHES, FLORIDA-69
BECKER, SCOTT-54,57
BEIJING CHAOYANG HOSPITAL-25,95
BIDEN, JOE- 17, 68
BIOMEDICAL ADVANCED RESEARCH-72
BIRX, DEBBIE-42
BLUNT, ROY-35
BOEING-43
BRIGHT, RICK-72
BRINKLEY, DOUGLAS-71

F's

FAST TRACK TESTING-53

FAUCI, DR. ANTHONY-V, 21, 41, 55, 58, 60, 61, 66, 71, 72, 81, 82

FDA-53, 54, 56

FEDERAL RESERVE-43

FIRST U.S. VICTIM-2, 48

FLORIDA-XIV, 57, 59, 69, 76, 78, 80, 86,

FLUSHING-11, 12

FORD, GERALD R.-36

FOREIGN CITIZENS ENTRY INTO U.S.-8, 22

FOX NEWS-22, 38, 58, 64, 75

FRANCE-XXII, 10, 46, 63, 80

FRIEDEN, THOMAS R. DR.-7, 42

G's

GENERAL MOTORS-43

GENEVA-20

GEORGE, ASHA-42

GEORGETOWN UNIVERSITY-21,84

GERMANY-X,4,46,63,80

GHEBREYESUS, TEDROS ADHANOM-33,64

GIROIR, BRETT-81,82

GLATTER, ROBERT-32

GLOBAL HEALTH THINK TANK ACCESS HEALTH INTERNATIONAL-5

GLOBAL RISK ASSESSMENT-5

GOLDMAN SACHS GROUP INC.-24

GOP LAWMAKERS-35

GOSTIN, LAWERENCE-84

GOTTLIEB, SCOTT-54, 59, 66

GRAHAM, LINDSEY-68

GRASSLEY, CHARLES E.-44

N95 MASKS-28, 29, 30
NATIONAL BIODEFENSE STRATEGY-84
NATIONAL EMERGENCY-81, 62
NATIONAL HEALTH COMMISSION-3, 8, 16, 25, 46
NATIONAL INSTITUTE OF HEALTH-21, 34, 72
NATIONAL PRAYER BREAKFAST-17
NATIONAL SECURITY COUNCIL-21, 41
NETHERLANDS-45
NEW DELHI-38
NEW HAMPSHIRE-XVIII, 51
NEW INFECTIONS-24, 45, 54, 67, 85
NEW JERSEY-XIV, XVI, 80
NEW YORK-XV, XVI, XVII, XX, 11, 12, 40, 44, 46, 49, 53, 54, 56, 57, 58, 59, 60, 65, 69, 70, 80
NEW YORK CITY-XVI, XIX, XX, 11, 42, 55, 56
NEW YORK CITY HEALTH DEPARTMENT-42
NEW YORK TIMES-IV
NEW YORK UNIVERSITY-12
NEW YORK'S LENOX HILL HOSPITAL-32
NEW ZEALAND-6, 23, 45
NIAGARA FALLS-12
NIGERIA-45
NOLAN, MELISSA DR.-32
NORTH KOREA-36
NUZZO, JENNIFER DR-21
NYC & COMPANY-12

O's
O'BRIAN, ROBERT-9
O'CONNOR, EILEEN-79
OBAMA ADMINISTRATION-22, 41, 83, 84
OBAMA, BARACK PRESIDENT-36, 42, 83
OMENKA, OGBONNAY-33

T's
TAIWANESE-23
TEST KITS-XI, 1, 51, 53, 55, 56, 57
TEXAS-X, 69, 70, 76, 86
THREE PHASE PLAN-III, V, 67
TOURISM ECONOMICS-11
TRAVIS AIR FORCE BASE-15
TRUMP ADMINISTRATION-V, XI, I, XXI, 1, 2, 3, 8, 11, 34, 35, 36, 37, 38, 39, 41, 42, 44, 46, 48, 50, 53, 54, 56, 59, 61, 62, 63, 66, 71, 72, 77, 78, 79, 81, 83, 84
TRUMP, DONALD-III, V, XI, XVII, XIX, XX, XXI, XXII, 1, 2, 17, 18, 33, 34, 38, 41, 42, 43, 46, 48, 62, 64, 67, 68, 69, 70, 71, 72, 76, 77, 79, 81, 83, 107

U's
U.K.-XXIII, 6
U.N.-7, 46
U.N. HEALTH AGENCY-4, 23
U.S. CHAMBER OF COMMERCE-14
UELAND, ERIC-46
UNION HOSPITAL-29
UNITED AIRLINES HOLDING INC.-6, 8
UNITED NATIONS SECRETARY-46
UNIVERSITY OF HONG KONG-10, 13, 24, 27
UNIVERSITY OF SOUTH CAROLINA SCHOOL OF PUBLIC HEALTH-32
UNIVERSITY OF WASHINGTON-50

V's
VIRGINIA-XVI, XVII, 61, 67, 64
VERMONT-XVIII, 69, 82
VIETNAM-4

Gerald L. Hutson Biography

Gerald has been married for 52 years and lives with his wonderful wife and family in Illinois. He enjoys the outdoors, boating and fishing with his wife and family of three children, two boys and one girl and eight grandchildren along with a young cattle dog and cat that keeps us all young. Gerald writes songs and plays the acoustic guitar and sings traditional songs and is asked occasionally to entertain. Every year Gerald plays Santa Claus for many children and adults at local local grade schools and businesses in which he plays and sings Christmas songs. Gerald served five years in the U.S. Air Force and received accommodation awards for writing and correcting Ground Communication Equipment manuals so that fellow airmen could follow operations without failure.

As Vice President of Operations, Gerald authored Quality Assurance procedures that established manufacturing criteria for customers. Gerald was a key contributor in development of the first integrated circuits in the 60's that replaced thousands of discrete devices in one small package. Gerald now enjoys his retirement with his family and friends.

Acknowledgments

Special thanks go to the support team of Andrea Kuzniar, Robert Horn, and Joey Rodriguez for their dedicated technical expertise in developing and enhancing the COVID-19 book. The typewritten manuscript was professionally typed, with twenty-two chapters, laid out, and edited by Andrea. The front COVID-19 cover which depicts in three words the progression of COVID-19 was designed with color enhancements by Robert Horn, a professional graphics designer, and professor at a local college. The technical graphs depicting the COVID-19 deaths in the United States, in chapter 22, showed the cycle of COVID-19 as the United States deaths cycled in a pattern going up and down for months. Hundreds of numbers were analyzed and collated by Joey and presented statistically so the reader could have a better understanding visually of the changing cycle of deaths in America!

Gerald L. Hutson

www.ingramcontent.com/pod-product-compliance
Lightning Source LLC
Chambersburg PA
CBHW071353280526
45787CB00001B/311